CREATIVE LIVES AND WORKS

Anthropologists of India

CREATIVE LIVES AND WORKS

Anthropologists of India

Adrian C. Mayer, M.N. Srinivas,
André Béteille and Jonathan Parry

In conversation with
Alan Macfarlane and Jack Goody

Edited by
Radha Béteille

SOCIAL SCIENCE PRESS

Published by
Esha Béteille
Social Science Press
69 Jor Bagh, New Delhi 110 003

ISBN: 978-93-83166-43-5

Set in Sabon Lt Std
Typeset by Manmohan Kumar, Delhi 110 035
Printed by Saurabh Printers Pvt. Ltd.

Contents

Transcriber's Note vii
Introduction ix

Anthropologists of India – Alan Macfarlane 1

PART I

Adrian Mayer – In conversation with Alan Macfarlane 9

PART II

M.N. Srinivas – In conversation with Jack Goody 51

PART III

André Béteille – In conversation with Alan Macfarlane 93

PART IV

Jonathan Parry – In conversation with Alan Macfarlane 131

Appendix: Biographical Information 171

Transcriber's Note

The transformation of videographed speeches into the written word has been a riveting experience. Transcriptions, while retaining the essence of a conversation, lend a new dimension to the oral transmission, opening them up to a wider readership, including those with diminished auditory functions.

This collection of transcripts tries to capture the engaging interactions between Alan Macfarlane, one of Britain's foremost social anthropologists, and the four eminent social anthropologists and sociologists – Adrian C. Mayer, M.N. Srinivas, André Béteille and Johnathan Parry. In fact, the intellectual discourses in these interviews on sociology and social anthropology draw in the reader as a participant. And, while offering a different order of internal cohesiveness, accentuates the ability of the reader to retain information, in this case, knowledge and scholarship.

The four transcripts offer similar, yet varied experiences. Adrian Mayer's recollection of his fieldwork days is captivating. M.N. Srinivas takes a few brief minutes to warm up before this interview becomes enlivening. André Béteille weaves in an occasional anecdote from his fieldwork experience while bringing out the subtle difference between social anthropology and sociology. Johnathan Parry recounts his journey into academia with an abundance of wry wit and humour.

Here, it must however be noted that not being a subject expert has been somewhat limiting because I have had to acquaint myself with speech patterns, accents, diction and intonations in areas that I was unfamiliar with when I began.

Furthermore, the transcribing of oral transmission leaves little room to represent facial expressions and non-verbalized sounds such as chuckles, laughs, sighs and for that matter exclamations, as well as pauses and idiosyncrasies in actual speech. Thus, I have taken the liberty to replace them with closely corresponding punctuations, so as not to alter the meaning or import of what is being said. Discrepancies in speech patterns have been isolated and addressed. Any misrepresentation of words and phrases is entirely inadvertent.

The trust and generosity of Professor Macfarlane in sharing his wealth of scholarship with Social Science Press cannot be adequately expressed in words.

– Radha Béteille
30 September 2020

Introduction

Alan Macfarlane

There have been many autobiographical accounts of the creative process in science as well as in the arts, humanities and social sciences. Yet these tend to concentrate on one level, and within that one aspect, the cerebral, intellectual working of a single thinker's mind. If we are to investigate further the connections between the levels of civilization, institution, network and individual, and the fifth dimension of chance or random variation, we need to supplement these accounts, in particular by letting scientists and others talk in a relaxed way about what they think has been important in their lives and works. Over the years I have been collecting such data and here I would like to describe how this happened and what opportunities it opens up for further understanding of the springs of creativity.

***

There is a puzzle as to why I have spent so much time and effort (and expense) on interviewing (on film) a large number of academics and others over the years. No one else has done this as far as I am aware and it has few tangible rewards except the occasional gratitude of one's colleagues. Why and how did this project build up over the years to a point where I now have about 250 lengthy interviews, almost all of them on the web?

One factor is clearly my anthropological training and the experience of anthropological fieldwork. Although some social historians of the recent past began to become interested in oral history and the tape recording of memories from the late 1960s, for example

Paul Thompson, Brian Harrison and others, on the whole historians deal with dead people who cannot be interviewed. Certainly, as a 17th century historian I was not interested in interviews.

Anthropologists, on the other hand, deal with the living and the 'life history' or in-depth study of one or two 'informants' naturally leads into the use of recording devices – again usually tape recorders, but also sometimes film cameras, to record interviews. So, from my first fieldwork in 1968–70 in Nepal, I was aware of the potential of interviews. Alongside the interviews with intellectuals described below, I have made in-depth interviews with my anthropological subjects, in particular a ten-part interview with Dilmaya Gurung in 1992. I also taped and filmed members of my family talking about their lives, especially my grandmother in 1978.

My interest in biographical details as a source of social history was also stimulated by the accident of moving through a number of different intellectual landscapes in my early years. My grandmother's stories of Burma and India and then my mother's vivid autobiographical writings in her letters and when she visited me from India were early influences which led to an interest in listening to older people talking about their lives. So, when I became an undergraduate and then a graduate at Oxford (1960–66) I spent some time listening to elderly academics, particularly my history tutor Lady Rosalind Clay with her deep immersion in the world of Oxford life through her father A.L. Smith (Master of Balliol), Sir Henry Clay, her husband and links to the Michison and Mitford families. She seemed to know personally many of the people whose books I was reading – Namier, Tawney, Trevelyan, Hill, Habakkuk, and she told me about their lives and personalities. I also began to hear about the folklore and gossip of historians from my other teachers – Harry Pitt, Keith Thomas and others.

The world of the historians was brought into relief by being on the edge of another group of academics, the social anthropologists. As I did my D.Phil. on witchcraft I began to meet the older members of the distinguished school of anthropologists, the Lienhardts, John Beattie and above all E.E. Evans-Pritchard. This was a particularly intense and gossip-connected tribe and I heard their stories of the great feuds and friendships and how they had survived their fieldwork.

The interest in biography was also strengthened by my early apprenticeship in history at Oxford where I was taught how important it was to study not only the works but also the lives of great historians – Gibbon, Macaulay, de Tocqueville, Bede and others. This led me much later in my life to write detailed studies of other major figures in books on Montesquieu, Adam Smith, de Tocqueville, Maitland, Fukuzawa and others which put a strong emphasis on the biography as well as the ideas.

As a social historian I wanted to get inside the mentality as well as the social structure of the past. As an undergraduate I had discovered that letters (Pastons, Stonors) and diaries (Pepys, Kilvert) were wonderful sources for social history. So, my first book was a study of the life of one individual *The Family Life of Ralph Josselin*, based on the diary of a 17th century clergyman. Henceforth I collected letters, autobiographies, diaries, travellers' journals and made a great deal of use of this biographical material in a number of my books.

The early experience of eavesdropping on what appeared to be a disappearing world of a certain academic endeavour in the pre-war world of Oxford history and anthropology, was reinforced by moving to the London School of Economics (LSE) for two years, where giants of the post-Malinowski generation, Raymond Firth, Isaac Schapera, Lucy Mair, were on the point of retiring. Then when I moved to the School of Oriental and African Studies (SOAS) I met another group of giants from a previous age, particularly Adrian Mayer and Christoph von Fürer-Haimendorf who became my supervisor.

When I moved as a research fellow to Cambridge in 1971, I encountered again several oral worlds which intrigued me. There were a new set of older anthropologists, Meyer Fortes, Audrey Richards, G.I. Jones, Edmund Leach, S.J. Tambiah, Jack Goody among them. And there were a group set of historians, in particular Peter Laslett and Tony Wrigley. A third world was that of King's College, where memories of the Bloomsbury era lingered on with Dadie Rylands, Peter Avery, Christopher Morris, Richard Braithwaite and others.

With six or seven sets of oral history washing through my life by the age of thirty it would have been a rather insensitive and myopic young scholar who did not realize that he was experiencing something special and perhaps something that should be recorded for posterity. I did not want to write a conventional history of academic disciplines, yet I had a sense that there were webs of ideas and connections which were carried by elderly individuals which should be recorded. They should be treated with the same respect and desire to save and document as was accorded to small oral cultures around the world whose myths, legends, rituals and folklore was carefully recorded by anthropologists.

It was perhaps a jumble of such motives, combined with friendship with the Director of the Cambridge University Audio-Visual Unit, Martin Gienke, which led to the first experiment to record academics on film. I had been asked to organize a series of seminars in history and anthropology in 1976–77 for the Economic and Social Research Council (ESRC) and this I knew would be a chance to gather together some of the leading thinkers in both fields. If they were coming for several days to Cambridge, might it not be an idea to film them, both as an archive for future generations and to show to students and colleagues who could not come to the meetings? So I organized the seminars and two were filmed. Amongst those attending were many younger scholars who would become well known – Maurice Bloch, Raphael Samuel, Keith Thomas, Keith Hopkins, Peter Burke, and a number of more senior figures in their prime such as E.P. Thompson, Edmund Leach, Maurice Godelier, Jack Goody, Arnoldo Momiliagno and Ernest Gellner.

I had assumed that this experiment, which is up on the web, would be repeated by others as the technology became better. Yet, to my knowledge, it has hardly ever been duplicated. One of the few instances when something similar was done was again an idea I had. When making a six-part series for Channel 4 on the history of the world over the last 10,000 years, we assembled five leading historians and they talked for two days about various aspects of the past. The whole was filmed and is also up on the web.

The next step was probably influenced by this early filming attempt. Jack Goody had been involved in the filmed seminar and five years later, with the help of the Cambridge linguist Stephen Levinson, he arranged three seminars where Meyer Fortes, Audrey Richards and M.N. Srinivas would be filmed talking about their lives and work. Jack Goody then retired, but continued to take an interest in the project and interviewed several others for me, including John Barnes and Jean La Fontaine.

In 1982 a portable video camera which took low-band U-matic was available and so I founded the Rivers Video Project with several of my PhD students, to experiment with the use of film in teaching and research in anthropology. Among the early projects were several biographical and archival films, including a film of Brian Hodgson and a long interview in June 1983 of my supervisor Christoph von Fürer-Haimendorf. The group also filmed my undergraduate lectures and some of the students made a film as part of their course on T.R. Malthus.

Now that I had started to film interviews, I could see the way in which my early interest in the gossip and interconnections of what was in effect a small tribe of British social anthropologists could be turned into a permanent record. The first interviews tended to be done by someone who knew the subject well – Goody in the cases above, Jean La Fontaine interviewing Lucy Mair, Caroline Humphrey interviewing Owen Lattimore. But gradually this faded away and I did nearly all the interviews and all the filming. About ten of the interviews were however done by friends and colleagues abroad and sent to me.

At first the focus was almost exclusively on anthropologists – with some sociologists who were also anthropologists such as André Béteille, John Barnes, Ronald Dore. Later it was extended to others in the general area of social sciences, more sociologists and some historians.

The filming continued to be done for the next ten or fifteen years on low-band U-matic and the tapes were stored away. It was not easy or necessary to edit them, but nor was it easy to show them, so very few were ever shown to students or colleagues. I looked at the collection as an archival collection, a time capsule of a vanishing world, which might be interesting in a hundred years time. That was assuming that it would be possible to play them. Already twenty years after they were made the tapes of the ESCR seminars were unplayable in Cambridge and had to be saved by the National Film Council.

Then a set of interconnected technological changes occurred which affected many of my projects. The internet and high-speed broadband made it possible to send films across the world. Large external hard discs and new compression techniques made it possible to store and edit the films. The arrival of a digital repository in Cambridge in 2004 made it possible to put up the interviews we had done until that date in June of that year, an idea first suggested by Mark Turin.

This development, which meant that the material could be appreciated by many more people, and the arrival of better cameras for the filming, meant that I began to increase the number of my interviews. By 2004 I had done about 30 interviews, by 2006 there were about 70 interviews and lectures. I described my project in relation to the arts, humanities and social sciences to some colleagues in King's College. The scientists Patrick Bateson and Herbert Huppert were excited by the idea and asked whether I could extend the filming to cover the natural and physical sciences.

I was surprised that very few people or organizations appeared to be doing the in-depth 'lives and works' kind of interviews I had undertaken for the immensely larger fields of the sciences. (Two sites which did have interviews on were that at globetrotter.berkeley and the Vega project at Sussex initiated by Harry Kroto). I was also hesitant about my ability to interview in fields about which I knew nothing. But they urged me to try and introduced me to a number of distinguished scientists. Shortly afterwards Gabriel Horn became an active advisor on the project as well.

I started gingerly with the scientists, filming Dan McKenzie with whom I shared a room in King's, the co-discoverer of tectonic plates and continental drift. It went well and I greatly enjoyed it. Pat Bateson then interviewed Gabriel Horn and I filmed another session with them talking about their partnership, and I interviewed

Pat Bateson himself. So I was now sufficiently confident to interview other scientists. Having broadened it beyond arts and social sciences, there was all the world which lay between, such as economics, psychology, philosophy and so on. There were also other interesting people I wanted to film – the Vice Chancellor Alison Richard, the ex-Cabinet Secretary Richard Wilson, the musician John Rutter, the sculptor Anthony Gormley.

In fact, the series broadened out not only into politicians and civil servants, but into many other fields. There are interviews on the performing and visual arts, crafts and skills (pottery, gardening, sculpture), law, journalism, literary criticism, business, exploration, publishing, the military, filmmaking, classics, archaeology, architecture and linguistics. Whenever I heard of or met someone who seemed to have made a creative contribution to the world, whether they were a road sweeper or a College butler, up to some of the most distinguished thinkers in the world, I would try to interview them. It is a wide spread.

So, from May 2007 when the first scientists were filmed, until September 2009 when I formally retired as Professor, I filmed something like another 80 interviews and the total now stands at about 250 films.

As far as I know this archive is unique and as a number of the major figures are dead and others are getting very old, so the interviewing cannot now be done. There are some small projects, sometimes influenced by our experiments, in Germany, the London School of Economics and elsewhere. Yet on the whole there is nothing quite like this.

***

Naturally the way in which I have done the interviews reflects both my own interests and my experience of what works. My central aim has been to let the speakers tell their own story, present themselves as they wish to do, without threatening or probing or adversarial questioning. Yet in doing so, and with a roughly chronological approach, I have been particularly interested in the question of what accidents, historical contingencies, or personal traits have influenced the subjects and sent them towards a particular career. In particular, what they do has contributed to their more creative and sometimes inspired work and innovation in their various fields.

From the very start of my interest in the oral history of my seniors and contemporaries, I have been keen to learn what I should do to make me as good an anthropologist and historian as possible. What are the craft skills and what are the ways of thinking and ordering one's life which will maximize the chance of making a serious contribution to our knowledge of the world? This early interest was heightened when I found myself in the incredibly privileged surroundings of Cambridge for forty years, surrounded by the ghosts of Newton, Darwin, Rutherford and many others.

The following describes the topics I have tried to cover in my interviews. On the surface, the interviews are almost unstructured and I avoid referring to a written questionnaire as this can distract from the spontaneity of the occasion. I encourage the interviewee to talk about whatever they would like. My role is similar to a psychiatrist's, that is to say to let the subject narrate their life, in particular in relation to the obstacles and encouragements to creativity and discovery. We tend to cover the following:

when and where born
ancestry – going back as far as they like, including occupation and temperament and possible effects of grand-parents, parents and siblings
first memories and hobbies as a child
first and subsequent schools, with important teachers, hobbies, subjects which gripped them, sports and games, music, special books
university and those who taught and studied with them and interests there
first research, supervisors, mentors, influences
jobs and career and travels through life, work abroad
colleagues, friends and network of workers, partners and children
methods of working and thinking

major achievements and problem-solving during life, how they occurred, including especially important bursts of activity
administrative tasks
teaching and supervising of students
effects of their work environment (laboratories, departments, Colleges etc)
philosophy and religion
political views and activities
advice for a young person starting out in their field
specifically ask if there is anything which they would like to have talked about and I have omitted to ask about

Yet if the subject does not want to follow this order, or to answer all of these, or to add further subjects, that is fine. What I want the reader to see is the inside of a life, told in a conversational and personal way.

***

The interviews are an intimate probing of personal experience, usually by a complete stranger who is holding a potentially threatening video camera. The subjects know that this may be seen by almost anyone in the world – friends, students, competitors, and enemies, now and in the future. This could be intimidating, especially to older subjects and for those who share a widespread reserve and distaste for talking about themselves.

I have, therefore, developed a number of techniques for putting the subjects at their ease. These have contributed, I believe, to the rather startlingly honest and trusting conversations which I have managed to have with a wide range of near strangers. It is worth briefly summarizing these since they could be helpful for others who help to extend this project.

1. It is important to have a fairly small and unostentatious camera that does not dominate or frighten the subject. The less intrusive the microphone the better – which is one reason why I have

given up using lapel microphones. I place the camera on my knees and do not use a tripod, which can again be intimidating.
2. The room in which the interview is done is important. I avoid formal settings if possible – lecture theatres, 'offices', and seminar rooms. A room with gentle furnishings, an easy chair for both interviewee and interviewer, books and pictures and objects in the background, a pleasant view all helps. And of course absolute silence and absence of telephones, mobiles, computers and interruptions is essential. I do not sit too close, or too far away. I sit at the same level, as I would do in any normal relaxed conversation between friends.
3. I try to develop the sheep-dog technique. When gently moving a flock of sheep to its destination, a good sheep dog is mostly silent and still. Each time the sheep move in a satisfactory direction, the dog creeps forward. And then sinks onto the grass and waits attentively. It does not bark, just guides. So, if possible, I try to help the interviewee along, but only interrupt when they need encouragement or direction. I never shut them off (though I occasionally warn them if the conversation is getting into the realms of damaging speech and check that they are aware of this), but try to bring them to subjects as they are needed.
4. I always try to show interest, however little I know, or even care about the subject being discussed. What is being said is often important to the subject and has a depth which I, or others, may only realize later. They deserve serious attention and respect for what is often a summary of a life. Of course, I may verbally disagree a little, or query things, but I try always to do so in the pursuit of a common goal of understanding. Curiosity is the most important attribute.
5. It is important for there to be no sense of rush. If I want an hour of film, I allow 90 minutes, which gives time for general conversation, a cup of tea etc.
6. I used to prepare carefully for the interviews. With people in my own subjects, this was possible. With scientists, beyond reading a brief life in an encyclopaedia, I cannot really prepare. It seems to work as well without preparation.

7. I used to think that it would be good if the 'subjects' prepared themselves in some detail, and when they asked me, I would advise this. In fact, I have found that spontaneity, even if it leads to some confusion, forgetting of names etc., is better and I advise people not to think about the interview – just that it will be chronological and they can say what they like (though they can look at one or two of the earlier interviews on the web if they would like to do so).
8. The fact that there is no commercial side to the endeavour has an effect. That I am doing it without specific pay for the job and not as part of a well-funded project, is usually obvious and helps. That all the materials are freely available on the web, can be downloaded for free anywhere in the world and used in teaching and research, all adds to the trust and spirit of altruistic collaboration.
9. The absence of any bureaucracy is important. We enter into an implicit contract. I have no paper for them to sign, assigning copyright, intellectual property rights etc. It is all agreed verbally and informally in the act itself. And hence the bond of friendship is not broken.
10. One of the things that has developed over the years and has greatly increased the interest and usability of the interviews is the possibility of putting up a summary with some time codes to help viewers navigate to an area that particularly interests them. The summaries are often very detailed and the development of the web has again made them more interesting and reliable since one can check names, theories, and connections. They also summarize much of the essence and flow of the interview. It is an art form in itself, combining considerable synthetic skills, a jigsaw ability and great concentration. It is not easy, but the website gives many examples of highly professional examples which have won high praise from the interview subjects who are often amazed at how accurate and complete they are. The obvious comprehension shown in the summary further adds to the sense of trust.

11. Before the interview it is important to explain that anything that is said can be retracted or glossed later. People should not censor themselves too much. Candour and a relaxed flow of ideas are important and trying to avoid things detracts from this. I explain that while filming – before or after saying something – the interviewee can easily say 'this is not for public dissemination', 'this is confidential' or whatever. Any such passage is then excised from the version that becomes publicly available – but the original tapes are kept for posterity. I also explain that we will send them the full summary which needs to be checked for accuracy (especially names and technical terms), interpretations of statements, and also gives the person a chance to withdraw any section or passage if they wish. They may, as has sometimes happened, feel that they want to add something – some more autobiography, a clearer exposition of something technical. It is not difficult to put this into the summary either in square brackets or as an appendix.
12. The duration of time people can concentrate varies. Most people can manage an hour, and then, with a break, another hour. When the tape ends I allow a few minutes for revival – but it is important not to lose the momentum. Some people prefer to do an hour, go away and come back some days later. This is alright, but can lead to repetition. But for older subjects (and many of mine are in their later eighties and older) it may be necessary. The older subjects also often feel more comfortable in their own homes amongst their books and belongings. This often gives an added dimension to the interviews.

If the subjects do reveal things which should be kept private for some years or even decades, these are edited out of the versions that go on the web, but the original tapes and full interviews will be preserved for posterity. Meanwhile the edited versions are put up on DSpace at Cambridge and on other websites, including YouTube, and now increasingly on websites all over the world – Scandinavia, America, China and elsewhere. The value of the interviews is enormously enhanced by the excellent and thorough summaries which Sarah Harrison has made of most of them, taking much more time and skill to do than the interviews themselves.

What has been created, through a set of accidents, is a resource for the study of a number of academic disciplines, from anthropology to molecular biology, from history to astronomy, from sociology to mathematics. It also provides rich material for the study of British academic life and institutions in the 20th century. Furthermore, for those interested in the conditions of creativity and discovery, it is a unique archive.

The project has developed as a result of a set of accidents and through the help and support of many people, in particular Sarah Harrison, Mark Turin, Jack Goody, Gerry Martin and many others. However, this project to publish the full interviews of selected individuals was the idea of Esha Béteille, whose support and advice have been indispensable. I would particularly like to thank Radha Béteille who it has been a great pleasure to work with. Her transcripts and editing have been extraordinarily well done and I am deeply impressed and grateful for her contribution. Institutions such as Cambridge University (DSpace and the Streaming Media Service in particular) and King's College, as well as the British Academy, the Leverhulme Trust, the Firebird Foundation and others have also made all this possible. It is hoped that others will take the task on through the 21st century.

Anthropologists of India

Alan Macfarlane

I was born in Assam, India, in 1941 and spent my first five years in India, learning Urdu and playing with Indian friends and looked after by Indian *ayahs*. As tea planters, my parents lived alongside various Tibeto-Burman tribal groups, including the Nagas and the matrilineal Garos and Khasis. In fact, my links with India go back through my mother's family to the late eighteenth century and my mother, and both her parents, were born in India or Burma. The personal link was deepened when I returned in 1968 to do fieldwork in neighbouring Nepal, where I have spent several years during twenty visits over a period of fifty years.

These strong family and personal ties made the anthropology of India important to me. This is re-enforced by the importance of India in the history of British social anthropology, and later American and French anthropology. Two of the first serious fieldwork-based studies in anthropology were made in India. The first was based on fieldwork among the Todas of central India in 1901–02 by W.H. Rivers, published as *The Todas* (1906). The second was A.R. Radcliffe-Brown's work in the Andaman Islands in 1906–08, published as *The Andaman Islanders* (1922), both preceding the work of Bronisław Malinowski.

The Nagas played a particularly important part in the early days of social anthropology. Two of the early colonial anthropologists, T.C. Hodson and J.H. Hutton became the first two Professors of Anthropology at Cambridge University and a third, J.P Mills, a Reader at the School of Oriental and African Studies. The finest collection of tribal artefacts from anywhere in the world in the Pitt-Rivers Museum at Oxford are from the Nagas.

Other notable explorers of the Nagas were my own supervisor, Christoph von Fürer-Haimendorf, who went to work in the Naga Hills in 1936. It was upon his work, and that of his friend Ursula Graham Bower, that we based our project on the Nagas, with a museum exhibition, videodisc containing film and photographs, a database of original materials and a book, written with Julian Jacobs. Both Haimendorf and Graham Bower are among the interviews in my collection. Thus, India shaped British social anthropology, particularly in the first phase of trying to understand tribal worlds on the edges of the expanding British Empire.

After the Second World War, anthropology moved towards the study of settled peasantries and literate civilization. Here again India was important, particularly in the work of American anthropologists. One example of this new interest is the work of McKim Marriott, whose interview is on my website.

There are a number of other interviews of people who worked on India or its peripheries. Edmund Leach and Nur Yalman both worked in Sri Lanka (Ceylon). Polly Hill later worked in India. Piers Vitebski worked in central India and describes this in a lecture. Rodney Needham worked in Manipur. Akbar Ahmed worked with the Pathans and wrote more generally about Islam.

Within this wider context, the four interviews published here represent several important features of the anthropology of India. The first is of Adrian Mayer, born in 1922, who I interviewed in 2017 when he was ninety-five. His excellent memory and lucidity are outstanding and the long-time perspective of his encounter with India, from when he came to work with famine relief in India in 1944, makes this a very unusual interview.

I first met Adrian when I went to do a PhD at SOAS in 1968. I was struck by his courtesy, his egalitarian attitude and generous treatment of everyone, including humble PhD students, and his obvious intelligence and enthusiasm. I was most influenced theoretically by his development of methods connected to the study of networks and quasi-groups. This was important in the 1960s and 1970s as anthropology moved from the study of bounded communities to the much more diffuse, fluid and complex world of large peasantries and urban societies.

The second interview is of M.N. Srinivas who was born in 1916 and recorded in a seminar organized by Jack Goody in 1982. Although the format is different and the technology in its infancy, it is an important record because of Srinivas' eminence as arguably the greatest Indian anthropologist. Srinivas had worked in an anthropological manner before the Second World War, but he then came to England in the 1940s and wrote his seminal work, later published as *Religion and Society among the Coorgs of South India* (1952), as a PhD at Oxford. He is best known for this work and more generally for his theories concerning caste mobility through the process of 'sanskritization', that is the adoption of higher-caste culture by socially mobile groups and individuals. This showed that caste was much less rigid than many had thought and the complex ways in which symbols could be used to manipulate social positions.

I met Srinivas, or Chamu as he was known, in 1982 when the recording was made. We note in our diary on 6 June 'Srinivas and my mother came to supper. He's a delightful and extremely intelligent man and it was a very nice evening'. I was to meet him again at a conference in Bangalore in 1995, when we visited his home city of Mysore. Alas, I failed to do an interview of him in the rush of the conference and the excitement of visiting the Nilgiri Hills where my grandfather had been born.

The third interview is of André Béteille. André was born in 1934 and is therefore seven years older than I am. Through the years we have had a close friendship since I first met him in 1978 when I note in my diary 'In the afternoon went to a seminar paper by A. Béteille on "Natural Inequality"'. Very good, showing that supposedly 'egalitarian' societies have ideas of 'natural inequality', he became like an older brother. We frequently met him on his academic visits to Cambridge over the years and I watched as he became the most senior sociologist/anthropologist (there is little distinction in India) in India, as head of the Indian Council of Social Science Research, Vice Chancellor of various universities and top Professor at the Delhi

School of Economics. It was to this institution that he invited me to give one of the three Silver Jubilee lectures at the Delhi School in 1999, alongside Amartya Sen and Srinivas. My wife and I stayed with André and his charming family several times in Delhi and he was always a great support and advisor.

André influenced my ideas mainly through his renowned work on equality and inequality, his edited collection for Penguin, *Social Inequality: Selected Readings* (1969). His application of some of the ideas from Alexis de Tocqueville to the Indian caste system was ground-breaking. André did a conventional anthropological field study, published in his *Caste, Class and Power: Changing Patterns of Stratification in a Tanjore Village* (1965), which was a set book in Cambridge for some years, it was his grander vision of caste and class comparatively across the world that influenced many of us. I presented my reactions to his ideas in an essay, 'Four systems of Stratification' in Ramachandra Guha and J. Parry (eds.), *Institutions and Inequalities in South Asia: Essays Presented to André Béteille* (1999).

One final debt I owe him is that he set me on the course to writing a many-volume autobiography. André's insight into equality and inequality, I have always assumed, is connected to the fact that there is a tension in his life between his French side (shown in his name and descent from a French father) and his Indian side. André decided to write a vignette of his grandmother and his early life. I read this and encouraged him to write more, which he did in his autobiography.

When André retired, a collection of accounts of the childhood of anthropologists, all of them except myself Indians, was published as 'Of Dragons, Hobbits and Anthropologists' in *Remembered Childhoods: Essays in Honour of André Béteille*, (eds.) Malavika Karlekar and Rudrangshu Mukherjee (2009). I found writing the article so interesting that I continued with the story, and have now published over 3500 pages, taking me to the age of thirty.

The last interview is of Jonathan, or, as he is widely known, Johnny Parry. Johnny was born in 1943 and read social anthropology at Cambridge and was supervised for his PhD by Edmund Leach. He was an exact contemporary of Caroline Humphrey, who also became a PhD student of Leach and whose interview, including some work in India, is on my website.

Johnny's original work was on *Caste and Kinship in Kangra* (1979). This established him as one of the finest ethnographers and anthropologists of India. I came to know him quite well through Cambridge and L.S.E. connections and interviewed him in late 2008.

The interview shows the careful, measured, balanced, thoughtful, gently humorous and warm individual whom I had come to know. Like me, he was strongly influenced by André. In particular, like André, he bridged the fields of anthropology and sociology. India is a vast, complex and anciently urban as well as rural civilization. Recently urban and industrial growth has been impressive and cannot be ignored by anthropologists. Much of Johnny's later work was devoted to the study of the mixed urban and rural, industrial and agricultural landscape. It shows how the fine-grained, participant-observation, approach can enrich the study of what is happening in India.

Johnny's work on the diverse worlds alongside the vast peasant population is complemented by one other interview, that of the leading anthropological film-maker David MacDougall. Famed for his early films in Africa and then Australia, in recent years David turned his attention to India. In several brilliant films, he has portrayed life in the institutions at the two extremes of Indian life. The first was the Doon School, the top Indian public (private) school, modelled on British public schools, and shown as an acclaimed series on television. (Incidentally, an interesting interview in my series is on Smo Das, a product of that school and later involved in the Tea business and married to a close Naga friend and advisor, Lily Das). The second was in a school in South India called the Rishi Valley School, a coeducational boarding school, based on the ideas of Krishnamurti. A third project involved filming and living at a shelter for homeless children in New Delhi.

PART one

Adrian C. Mayer. Photograph courtesy Alan Macfarlane.

Adrian C. Mayer

Emeritus Professor Adrian Mayer was awarded an Honorary Fellowship at SOAS after almost 30 years at the School. He joined SOAS in 1956, and was the first Chair of the South Asia Centre where he held the Chair of Asian Anthropology, later holding roles as Head of Department and finally Pro-Director before retiring in 1985.

Professor Mayer first went to India during the Second World War as a member of the Friends' Ambulance Unit, working in Bengal and Madras for two years. He subsequently trained as a social anthropologist at the London School of Economics, gaining his PhD in 1953 with a thesis on the Indian community in Fiji. Professor Mayer then took a research fellowship at The Australian National University, following which he joined SOAS.

Professor Mayer received the Rivers Memorial Medal from the Royal Anthropological Institute, served as the Institute's President from 1983 to 1985 and earlier edited Man, the Institute's journal. He was a member of the Social Science Research Council from 1973 to 1979. His publications result from research trips to India, Pakistan, Canada, Japan and Fiji.[1]

Some of Mayer's major books include, Caste and Kinship in Central India: A Village and its Region *(1960)*, Land and Society in Malabar *(1952)*, Indians in Fiji *(1963)*, India: Colours and Shadows of Spirituality *(2007) and* Peasants in the Pacific *(2013)*.

Alan Macfarlane (AM): It is a great pleasure to have a chance to talk to Adrian Mayer, one of my former teachers and inspirations. Adrian, when and where you born?
Adrian C. Mayer (ACM): I was born within a sea lion roar of the London Zoo in Cumberland Terrace, one of the nice terraces in Regents Park.

AM: And when was that?
ACM: That was in 1922, I shall be 95 in three weeks' time.

AM: So, it's in October?
ACM: No sorry it's a bit later than that, I'll have to cut that bit out! In December, it's in December. Three months' time, not three weeks.

AM: That's fine. Though you were born actually in the same year as my mother, but you are a few months younger.
ACM: Is that right?

AM: Few months younger. It's always interesting to know about anthropologists' ancestors and some people like to go back a few generations, but some just go back to their grandparents. Could you tell me something about your ancestry?
ACM: I'm a first-generation immigrant. Probably under Brexit[2] I would have to register or something in some way. My father came from Germany, from Mannheim. His father was a hop merchant, I remember him saying he was the first person to sell German hops to Guinness in Dublin. He died in his early fifties of diabetes before they had discovered insulin, so I never knew him. My father came here in 1896 to work with the firm of an uncle of his, his *Mama*, his mother's brother or uncle, perhaps, who was a Seligman, a family with wide interests in Britain and America. He started off at the bottom of the scale. His first job, I remember him telling me, was to undo the parcels that came into the office so that the string could be used subsequently.

This interview was conducted by Alan Macfarlane on 15 September 2017. The transcription for this interview was provided by Radha Béteille, for this volume. These interviews are available for viewing on:
https://sms.csx.cam.ac.uk/media/2575952
https://www.youtube.com/watch?v=fg2tGO0hdII

When he was in Mannheim he was something of a child prodigy as a pianist. He played the piano, there was a lot of music in Mannheim in those days and one of the family myths, that may possibly be true, that when Brahms[3] came to visit the city there was a concourse between the little boys as to who would play for the great man. My father came second because, he must have been eight or nine at the time, his feet couldn't reach the pedals; Brahms is said to have taken him on his knee and said, 'There, there little man. Next time you will play'. He naturalized himself in 1905 and lived for the rest of his life here.

AM: What did he do for the rest of his life?

ACM: He started off in a firm which was trading in non-ferrous metals. He worked his way up. He must have been quite good at it because when the War came he was in a reserved occupation because this was key stuff. They were importing nickel, lead and stuff for making munitions. In 1917 this was lifted, he joined a regiment which consisted of anyone with a German name, so bakers and butchers from Manchester, young men who didn't speak German, they were put in this and people like my father, of course.

It was the 31st Middlesex Regiment[4] and it was known as the Kaiser's Own. They were sent to the North Weald[5] to dig ditches and things like that. One day he was working fairly near the railway line and all his friends from the Stock Exchange in the carriage were looking at him and waving to him on their way to the city to continue their work. He continued with his musical interest. He got the local Commandant of the R.A.F. station there to transport his piano out so he could have trios and quartets in the camp because a lot of people there were like him. They were stockbrokers and amateur pianists and so on.

He met my mother at a concert in London – he was probably AWOL [Away Without Leave] at the time. She was the daughter of a civil servant who rose to be Chief Accountant at the War Office. They didn't mince matters there – they called a war a war! It was in the ministry's office in those days.

Her mother came from Ireland, but her father was either a man of Kent or a Kentish man. I forget how Kent is divided, one side of the county or the other. When she was in her late teens, she more or less ran away from home and became a singer. She sang for the Carl Rosa Opera Company.[6] She didn't have a very big voice but she sang the second role, the supporting role. Then later on, she became a lieder singer and sang lieder, so we were a musical household.

My parents entertained foreign musicians when they came over to London. My father's best friend was Artur Schnabel[7], the pianist, who used to stay with us. That was the setup for the later development of the children's concerts which he started in 1923 which became a whole movement as concerts for children in 23 or 24 centres, from Tyne Side down to Plymouth.

AM: This was Schnabel?
ACM: No, no. My father did this. They were called Robert Mayer Concerts for Children.[8] They had Malcolm Sargent[9] who was very personable and dynamic as conductor, who explained the pieces to the children before they were played. There was no compromise, they played a movement of a Mozart[10] concerto and didn't pander or try to popularize it at all, and the children accepted it, of course, why not?

AM: What was the character of your parents? How would you describe them as people?
ACM: My father was an organizer, a net-worker. With great difficulty did he get this movement started because there wasn't much music in the schools in those days. Somehow, he had to enthuse the heads, the music teachers, and then the County Councils and education authorities to send deputations from the schools to these concerts. There was a series of five or six in each season. He called himself a Tolstoyan.[11] I don't think he ever went to a synagogue. I don't think my grandfather did either actually. My mother was in a way a deeper musician than he was.

AM: Was she Jewish?
ACM: No, no, she wasn't at all. She couldn't live without music, there's no doubt, and she was a much more emotional person than my dad. I think my father left the upbringing of the kids to her.

AM: Did you have brothers and sisters?
ACM: I had a brother and a sister, yes. From her Irish grandmother, and also from the fact that she became very interested in the whole Suffragette movement.[12] She was a Suffragette here, and with the Irish renaissance.[13] I think the opera company went to Dublin in about 1910, so she met J.M. Synge,[14] Jack Yeats,[15] Willie Yeats,[16] Maud Gonne,[17] and all these people. It must have been a very exciting time to be in Dublin in those days.

AM: What is your first memory?
ACM: My first clear memory is of the 1926 General Strike[18] because, living in Regents Park, of course we had no traffic, no buses passed, but they must have had a bus park up near the Zoo, where now there's a big parking space and they must have put all the buses there, ready for these young university volunteers to drive them because I remember looking out of the window and seeing these buses pass us.
Buses in those days were private. The biggest company in those days was the General Bus Company which was red, that is why when it was nationalized, they were the red buses. Thomas Tilling[19] was mauve, I think, and there were lots of others, of course. The tickets were different, so we boys always wanted to travel on them. They were called pirate buses and we wanted to travel on anything that wasn't red. Looking out of the window and seeing these buses of different colours going past....

AM: So, you were about four?
ACM: I suppose I was four then. I also have a vague earlier memory of having an apple peeled for me. It must have been for my tea, perhaps I was sitting in a high chair. My memories of the past are not very detailed actually. Some people have photographic memories.

AM: What was your first school?
ACM: First school was a Montessori school, a little bit off beat you see. Then I went to a prep school which had a thing called the Dalton Plan[20] where you were responsible for planning your own work. You had a chart, you had to fill up all the spaces of all the subjects eventually, but you could decide how you did it, which

subjects you did first, the one's you liked or the ones you didn't, so it was much more flexible than a form system.

AM: That was a preparatory school?
ACM: That was a prep school.

AM: And it was a day school?
ACM: No, no, it was a boarding school. No, no, no. I suppose I was eight or nine.

AM: Where was that?
ACM: It was in Surrey where all the prep schools tend to be.

AM: What was it called?
ACM: It was called Abinger Hill. I haven't kept up with anyone from there. Too long ago.

AM: Did you basically hate it or enjoy it?
ACM: I liked it. I had one or two good friends. No, no, it worked out well. I was, of course, homesick for a few days before I went back, but I think maybe everyone probably was, didn't want to go back. But once one was there it was okay.

AM: You weren't bullied?
ACM: No, no. One or two people were bullied a bit, but heavy teasing, I supposed, is how one would call it, nothing like the cyber bullying you read about now where people's confidence is completely shattered by anonymous tweets.

AM: Were you particularly interested in any particular subject at that age or…?
ACM: No. I learnt Latin from the age of eight, I learnt Greek from the age of ten. We learnt two languages, three languages. There is something I should possibly mention too, is that my first language is French. My nanny – you had nannies in those days, my nanny was French. I should have asked my mother more about this, how long she was there, but she must have been there over the time when I learnt to speak, because I spoke to her and I spoke in French, that went on and she must've left. And then, I suppose, there was an English nanny, so for six months or more I spoke a language which was half English and half French and

no one could understand me at all! Later I must have decided, no, I'm an English boy and then we used to go to France from the age of about eight, even, about 1925–26. I think my parents were exceptional in those days, parents tended to go off on their own, and they left the kids to go to Birchington[21] or Littlehampton[22] or somewhere they could go with the nanny, but they took us down. I refused to speak any French because I was a little English boy. There are some atavistic words of French that ring a deep bell from my earliest consciousness, and I love speaking it and am very fond of France.

AM: Were you any good at any games, I mean that's sometimes....
ACM: No, no. Not really.

AM: Never have been?
ACM: No. When I went to public school, I went to a place called Bryanston....[23]

AM: Oh yes, very famous.
ACM: ...which again is off-beat. The system of working is the same with these charts where you decide when you do it. There I was an oarsman. I love rowing and they have a river there. They have bumping races and so on, and that was my sport.

AM: How was that school? Did you enjoy that at all?
ACM: Very much so. Yes, yes. At first, I was a cox and when I grew older, I was a stroke, but I was never in the top rank.

AM: In general, you liked the school.
ACM: Yes. Oh yes, absolutely. We had a remarkable headmaster, Thorold Coade,[24] was a very exceptional person. He gave people a lot of responsibility for themselves.

AM: Were you a prefect?
ACM: I don't think I was. I'm not a great leader in that sort of way.

AM: Were you engaged in any particular thing like debating or....
ACM: Yes, oh yes. My parents gave me one of the first so-called noiseless typewriters, and myself, Michael Howard[25] the historian, he was a co-eval of mine, and two or three others, we organized a newspaper. It was called the *Abinger News* or something. You ask

him, he'll be able to tell you and we had a debating society. We reported on the debates and all this sort of thing in this newspaper.

AM: Did you have any particular hobbies either at the preparatory or the public school? Did you collect things, or fish or...?
ACM: Oh, the usual cigarette cards and stamps. I'm not a collector. On the whole, if I go to some place, I have to buy presents to take home but I don't collect for myself, which is sometimes a shame because one has been to places where there were lovely things one could have bought to beautify. On the other hand, there is always a problem. Rajasthan, in the early '50s, people were cutting out miniatures out of books and selling them. Somehow, I took a principled stand that if I took them, they would cut out some more. Actually, the result was the same as if I hadn't done it.

But now when I see these paintings that I could have they would have been rather nice on my walls. When I was in Fiji, we were offered a whale's tooth which has a great ritual significance and there were various articles that were being sold for tourism, we were offered this to take home as a curio, we refused it.

AM: Did you have any other hobbies, were you interested in natural history, fishing or any kind of anthropological investigations of other cultures or anything else?
ACM: I was exposed to other cultures. We were exposed to all the customs, when we went as a family driving through France in an old Morris Cowley in 1926–27, on roads which were curved so we were always trying to keep on the crown of the road, in small hotels. When we got to where were staying, it was a place called Cavalaire,[26] which is quite near St Tropez which in those days was just a little fishing village. In Cavalaire, we made friends with a French family there and if we were swimming, they came and swam, and we had to shake hands under water, and you had to shake hands! I don't suppose it happens now. So, it's an example of...some were different.

AM: Other cultures. Were there any teachers at either of your schools who you remember as influencing you much? Inspiring you in any way?

ACM: The first school. I'm trying to remember the Headmaster. He was a very dynamic person. In Bryanston, my House Master, I suppose, was an influence on me, but basically the Headmaster. The influence of this man Coade was very strong in the school. There were very few rules, it was up to you, and you were responsible for yourself and you were responsible for the community. If you did something really, really bad, getting drunk on Dorchester cider[27] or something like that then instead of the uniform which was a pale blue, you had to wear a white shirt.

AM: Was there any beating?

ACM: No, no beating. No fagging. Nothing like that. It was a new school. It was started in around 1926 or 1928. Stowe was another school I think which was founded in the interwar period. There were one or two others which were non-traditional in that sort of way.

AM: What subjects were you specializing in the A-level.

ACM: I liked geography very much. That was my best subject, I loved geography. Language, I was a bit naughty with my French because since I knew it by ear, I didn't learn all the rules, so when it came to an exam paper, I tended to fly by whether it sounded all right or not. Later I learnt German too, dropped Greek but kept on Latin, of course you had to take the Latin, 'Little Go' and that sort of thing.

AM: You mentioned 'Little Go',[28] where did you go after?

ACM: I went to college in America, because I was there with my brother, my brother was American and he was at Harvard. I went over at the end of the summer term on a tour to see the country together. We were both there when the War was declared. I was 17 at that time, so I stayed on and went to college in America.

AM: Where did you go?

ACM: A place called St John's College at Annapolis in Maryland. There again it was an off-beat education, a liberal arts college, which they don't have here, but that's what they call them there. It was based on a wide variety of books – texts really. You learnt some Natural Science, you started with Euclid[29] and ended with Lobachevsky,[30] so from Euclidean to non-Euclidean. You had a different language each year, and then philosophers, and historians and so on. It was a wide, non-specialized education.

AM: You couldn't say this was a degree in X or...?

ACM: Not really, no. But in America you could say it was a degree in Liberal Studies, the quadrivium and the trivium[31] – it's a bit of both. Then I came back here. My mother ran the religious side of the family and she went steadily from being a non-conformist, a congregationalist, steadily downhill you might say, until she ended up with the Quakers.[32] You can't get much further than that! She might have tipped over to Unitarianism[33] or, I suppose, but she didn't. We were brought up in my final years as a Quaker. When I came back here, I joined the Friends Ambulance Unit[34] which was the Quaker ambulance unit which had actually started in the First War.

AM: That was 1942?

ACM: That was in 1943. We were given a training, worked on wards, ordinary wards. Then I had three months in an operating theatre, laying out trays for surgeons and counting the swabs so that bodies before you sewed it up. That was extremely interesting because there was a very well-known surgeon. It was in St James's Hospital, Balham. He was doing the first gastrectomies where you were taking the stomach out or taking bits of it out. You'd be surprised to learn that now they put a camera down your oesophagus to see about ulcers. But in those days, you put the tube down and there was someone who made a little water colour, there was a light, I can't be imagining this surely. He made that so that the surgeon could see the amount of dead tissue and how much he had to resect it. From then we had to learn to drive an HGV [Heavy Goods Vehicle], then we were attached to an RAMC unit[35] which itself formed part of the Fourth Armoured Division up in Northumbria. We learnt how to put up field stations in the middle of the night.

In 1944 we were all getting ready for D-Day[36] and all of a sudden, I got a letter to say I was going to India. These things happened suddenly in big old bureaucratic organizations so then I went to India and spent two years there.

The Friends' Ambulance Unit there was not doing that sort of medical work but doing relief and rehabilitation. First, I was in Bengal, the famine had finished but there was a big programme of drug distribution still.

AM: Was the effect of the famine still visible?

ACM: Yes. Of course. I don't know about Bengal, we didn't distribute milk there, to the weaker sections of society. But we distributed the first out sulphur drugs which had just come onto the market and things like Hexylresorcinol[37] which was for, oh, I forget what it was for now. My job, I was about 21 years, was to go around these districts.

AM: Were you in Calcutta?

ACM: I was based in Calcutta, but I spent a lot of time in the districts, going to hospitals, looking at the books to try to see whether the place was ship-shape. You couldn't really tell how much of the stuff was going to the black market, but just someone coming and asking for the books was some sort of a break. I did that for several months in the very beautiful country of East Bengal, now Bangladesh. There were very few roads in those days and you used river boats which stopped every two or three miles and people got on or off. Then in south India, in Kerala in the old Madras Presidency,[38] not the princely state part of Kerala, there was a programme, there was milk distribution for the weaker sections of society. I took over from someone and did it for about eight months from my base in Kozhikode (then Calicut).

Then I came back to Bengal, to Calcutta. We had a centre there, and worked. People were very afraid of famines because of the Bengal history. In the beginning of 1946, people were very afraid in South India of a food shortage that could develop into a famine.

They asked the Government of India could they send someone to help in this. The unit with this reputation of relief work was asked. I'd been in South India so they said, 'Let's send Mayer down'. I went down to Madras and, I helped set up with the Government a programme which took in the 10 deficit districts of the Presidency, I think we were giving milk and then some multi-vitamins to about 1,500,000 children. We were importing it from the States, then it had to be landed, it had to be put on trains, and taken up and then of course it had to be distributed.

While the thing was being set up and while the stuff was coming out, I went out, got hold of a jeep and went out to all the sub-districts to the *tehsildars*,[39] to apprise them of the situation. And if you met someone then he'd remember it. If it's just a piece of paper, he won't really look at him very much. The Collectors were the same. Once the stuff had started rolling out, by then I had two helpers, we toured around, so I got to know South India very well. It was very beautiful in those days.

I kept a diary and two years ago one of my Indian 'nieces' who is in Bombay, she said, 'Let's go down to South India'. She had a factory down there for handloom. 'Come on you haven't been down for some time.' So, we went down and drove around some of the districts which I had been in. It was different and I wondered why? Very obvious. In those days the road was gravelled, so it wasn't tar, it was the same colour as the fields. There were no advertisements, there were almost no houses between villages and between towns – there was nothing. So, you looked at nature and my diaries are full of the changing colour of the soil, the clouds change all sorts of natural features which nowadays you don't have, you whiz between one place and another. Petrol stations in every corner.

AM: Did you start learning the language, any other language?
ACM: No. Somehow, I wasn't there long really, because everyone was speaking English that I was talking to. I learnt a little Bengali, I learnt a little Malayalam, I learnt a little Tamil. I had the books and so on, but it didn't take off. It wasn't fieldwork in that sort of way.

AM: Then you came back, '46.
ACM: Then at the end of '46, I got a job as assistant to the Secretary General of the Institute of Pacific Relations. This was an outfit based in New York but was international. The British part of it was Chatham House, the Royal Institute of International Affairs. They were having a conference in September 1947 on the future of the Pacific region. A New Zealander, a very affable person, Bill Holland, he needed an assistant who would do a bit of legwork so he got to know of me and, I forget how, but any way, he appointed me. He said, 'We will meet in Manila but you better go to Bangkok and see who's there, see if there's anyone who can give a paper'.

So I was shunted to...and in those days when I was told I was going to Siam it was like I was going to the moon because no one went to places like that. It was really exciting, very exciting indeed. Nowadays you're in Bangkok and the terminal is exactly the same as the one you've left.

I went there in one of the old flying boats which was linking London and Sydney. It took seven days since they had the same crew, because they had only one crew since there was only one a week, so they flew between 8 o'clock in the morning and 4 o'clock in the afternoon, then they had tea, then a nice rest. We started off on the Hooghly then landed on the Irrawaddy and had some lunch, then we landed at, I forget what it was called, in Bangkok the river, and then they all went off for a decent evening. I went there and I went to Hong Kong and looked at the universities in Guangzhou, in Canton as it was then, staying on Xiamen Island[40] which was a foreign concession. Sturdy houses, rather like St John's Wood, a leafy place.

AM: Xiamen? Xiamen is the island with a university beside it.
ACM: That would be it. Later they had built an enormous hotel there. I went in 1985, looking down the Pearl River, it was very pretty. I went to Manila and met Holland and then we went to Shanghai and he had to go home as there was crisis in the organization so I carried on to Beijing.

AM: This was 1948?
ACM: This was 1947.

AM: This was 1947 and the war was still going on in China.
ACM: Oh yes. We had to fly because the Communists were between Shanghai, Nanking and Beijing, so there was no other way, they were connected by sea, I suppose. Shanghai was a disturbed place and these soldiers, I don't know how they were paid, because there was rampant inflation. If one really had to take some kind of sum of money out you took a suitcase, literally, to the bank.

AM: It was under the Kuomintang?[41]
ACM: Yes, this was under the Kuomintang. The soldiers, they would just get on a bus and push the people out. If we were riding on the bus, we were pushed out too.

AM: Was there great poverty?
ACM: Yes. Oh yes. But on the other hand, the people sitting on the pavement selling soup, the soup smelled so good. Then when I got to Beijing, we had several feasts and that was 20–25 courses or so.

AM: Do you have memories of Beijing when you went there?
ACM: Yes, yes.

AM: It hadn't been pulled down by then?
ACM: They closed the gates every evening so the Communists couldn't get in. And the first thing I did, this was February–March, I went down to this street of the silk vendors and got myself a long gown, because everyone was in these long gowns as it was pretty parky at that time.

My diary – for instance, I went from there to Tientsin,[42] it's called something else now, and saw the universities there, and coming back you came across the flat land and then you see Beijing, you see the Temple of Heaven[43] and you see the mountain with the Tibetan Monastery – that was all there was. There were no high buildings at all. It meant that the Forbidden City and Temple of Heaven were part of the city.

AM: Did you go on to the Forbidden City?[44]
ACM: Oh yes. It was free, and it had all the beautiful works of art which I then later had to go to Taiwan to see. They took them all away with them. But they were all organic parts of the city. Now I would imagine they are like some cities that we know where they just stand up as special places.

AM: Like the Drum Tower.[45]
ACM: Yeah.

AM: Was there great poverty there as well?
ACM: I don't know. I can't remember in Beijing. When I had done all the interviewing I had a couple of weeks before I travelled back to San Francisco on a troop ship and I had a couple of weeks so I went to…we had a unit in the Friends' Ambulance Unit in China and during the war it had been transporting along the Burma Road[46] relief supplies and things. Then they started a rehabilitation centre in Hunan so I thought I would go and have a look at the

countryside a bit. It was hair-raising because I didn't know a word of Chinese and from Nanking you had to go north on a railway to a place called Suzhou then you joined the Belgian-built railway which went to the west. I arrived in Suzhou[47] at about 10 'o' clock at night not knowing where to put up and what to do. Somehow, I managed to make myself understood, I can't remember how, I was put in a hotel which was absolute bedlam because it turned out to be a bawdy house. And the whole night, there were fights between the clients who said they hadn't been served enough and the ladies who said they had given them too much!

At about 5.00 or 6.00 in the morning, I got away and went to the station and there was an old boy who talked some French from the time the Belgians built the railways, must've been the last person. So somehow, I managed to get a ticket. It was a disturbed time and the stations were little fortresses.

AM: Did you come close to the Communists?
ACM: The Communists were only 30–40 miles away to the north; it was just on the way to Yan'an.[48] In the village, having seen Indian villages, they didn't look as poor because if you have someone all someone who is in a *dhoti* or a *lungi*.[49]

AM: Were they eating...reasonably?
ACM: Yeah. We had to have *mantou*,[50] that steamed stuff, very simple of course. All these myths about Chinese meals where they have lots of meat and pork....

AM: Were you on your own there as a Westerner in this village?
ACM: No. no. They had a team there, in fact some of them were Friends from England and I stayed there for five or six days. So, I did see a little bit of China before going back to the States and worked in the office there in New York and then back to England and worked at Chatham House to organize this conference.

AM: This was in '48?
ACM: Held at Stratford which was quite difficult because of transport problems. This was at the end of 1947. This was where I met a fellow anthropologist or soon to be a Fellow, Cyril Belshaw,[51]

who was representing New Zealand at this conference. Later, I told him that I was learning Hindi at the School of Oriental and African Studies (SOAS)[52] rather I felt this was unsatisfactory. I was just learning the language – I wasn't learning anything about the society. He said, 'Well come down to the LSE and meet Raymond Firth[53] and he might suggest something to me'. I went and Raymond was very affable and asked me, 'What would you like to go to?' He presented me with a list of seminars, there was a seminar on cultural change. I think I told you this story. So, I said, 'Well this looks interesting on cultural change'. I went to it and it was the famous Malinowski[54] seminar; after two or three weeks, Raymond asked me, 'Mr Mayer, how are you getting on? I said, 'It sounded very interesting but I can't understand much of it'. He laughed and he said. 'You better start at the beginning'. So, I registered for the Diploma.

AM: Who were the teachers on the Diploma?
ACM: Nadel,[55] Leach,[56] Audrey Richards.[57]

AM: Could you give us a pen portrait of the three you've mentioned.
ACM: Nadel, of course, I worked with him in Canberra afterwards. He was quite strict. You must have read the books – severe anthropologist.

AM: Yes. Severe anthropologist.
ACM: Exactly, very severe and he turned out to be, in Canberra, fairly severe, unlike Australians who tend to be easy-going; Leach taught me primitive technology. Why would he do that?

AM: He worked on Malaya. His first work was on Malay canoe construction if you remember.
ACM: I don't remember that.

AM: What was your impression of him?
ACM: He wasn't sort of flights of fancy, you can't get very far when you're talking about canoe-building or whatever. I think he taught me about fieldwork. One thing he didn't say, 'Don't lose your field notes'. Poor chap had lost his. Highly approachable. Richards was all African and I hadn't been to Africa and I didn't really....

AM: What was Audrey like?
ACM: Audrey wasn't inspiring, but then she was talking about age sets etc., things that didn't interest me much.

AM: Not about her nutritional work, not about her diet or…?
ACM: No. Not that I recall.

AM: Was there anyone inspiring as a lecturer?
ACM: Raymond was the best lecturer. Schapera[58] was there. I was interested and highly interested and of course I was very motivated to get this thing, though I didn't think that I would then become an academic at all. Ian Hogbin[59] came. There were a lot of people that came to the seminar when they were in London. Ian Hogbin, we must have talked, and Raymond mentioned me and Hogbin said. 'If he wants to study Indians let him go to Fiji'. I was in for a Horniman scholarship and I went to see J.H. Hutton.[60]

AM: Really?
ACM: Not a million miles from where we are sitting [in King's College]. He was the only person that I have met who actually had a nightcap on. He must have had flu or something. He was sitting there. He had a goatee.[61]

AM: In the museum, in our museum probably.
ACM: Well it was Sydney's bedroom. I had an idea of going back to Kerala because I knew it a bit. It was a lovely place. He said, oh yes, you should study the Mukkuvas', the fishermen down on the beach. I had an idea of going to the Laccadives[62] because one of my friends was the sub-divisional officer and he had to go there once a year. And Hutton said, No, no, no. You study the Mukkuvas'. I did not like the idea of living on a beach with the constant smell of rotting fish 24 hours in the day. Luckily Harry Powell got the grant to go to the Trobriands[63] and then I had to cast around and then Raymond came up with this idea of Fiji. Why not?

AM: Was this to do a doctorate?
ACM: Yes, this was for my doctorate, and I did it under Raymond because though the ANU[64] [Australian National University] gave me the grant for the scholarship, there weren't any professors in

Canberra at that time. Nadel had not come out. In fact, by then I was married and we got out to Canberra and the ANU was just a single wood shed. At one end was the Vice Chancellor and at the other end was the Bursar. I had a couple of months in the Mitchell Library going through the colonial papers, the Fiji Papers, but the first few days we spent in Canberra. When we were leaving, Copland,[65] who was Vice Chancellor, said to Bill Hamilton, 'How much do you think we should give him for living expenses?' I don't know. It was done on the back of an envelope.

AM: Was it enough?

ACM: It was enough. I don't think they realized how frugally one does live in the field.

AM: What was the theme or subject that you were going to study?

ACM: It was just how the society worked. The Indians came out on a 10-year indenture, five years of which they spent working in a barracks working for the sugar mill company. After that they were given a plot of land if they wanted to stay and they were peasant farmers, contracted to sell their cane to the mill, the Australian company mill – a big company called The Colonial Sugar Refining Company which had the monopoly. They were recruited from Hindi speaking areas in eastern U.P., which has always been a very poor area, and Bihar, about two–thirds and one–third from the South. So, there were some Tamil speakers, there were not many Malayalam speakers. There were Tamil speakers, 25 per cent and the rest Hindi speaking Bhojpuri or speaking Maithili, and different castes; recruiters might pick up runaway people at railway stations and bazaars and told them there was a job in a place called Fiji, and where is it, it is quite near Calcutta.

They were taken down to Calcutta and then on ships. On the ship, of course, you couldn't have caste distinctions, all this business about eating together or eating from each other's plates and kitchens and all the rest of it simply collapsed. What happened when they got access to Fiji, they were put into lines, again caste was not a criterion, but when they had finished, most of them stayed on in Fiji. What kind of society did they recreate? So that was basically what I wanted to study.

AM: What did you find. What was your main finding?
ACM: I found that there was in fact very little institutional organization. The only hard and fast one was the gang of cane cutters in a particular area. There were no divisions into villages, no centres in villages. I had been in Malabar which has non-nuclear settlement, but every house was on its little patch of 10-acre cane, with maybe a store at the central crossroads. There was a tendency for cultural groups to gather in one particular area, South Indians here, Muslims here, Hindi speakers here and so on. But there was no formal organization – no Panchayat or anything like that at all.
AM: Was there intergroup marriage?
ACM: No. Good Lord, no! Different linguistic groups, even within, there were people from lower castes and also people from higher castes and there wasn't any intermarriage, it was very *sub rosa*, no one talked about that. You had to derive that from certain rituals they might say or their names, it was all under the earth.

The only institution was the cane-cutting gang that took in 75 per cent of the homesteads, because not all had land. The cane-cutting gang had a *sardar*[66] who, I don't think it was a former election, I'm not quite sure, I can't quite remember, but he was recognized by the company. The company had an overseer in each sector who ran the thing, and he ran it very well, he was very paternalistic. He told them what seed to put in, and he would've controlled, I would've thought, and the number of ratoons.[67] After you cut the cane if you leave it, you'll get another growth and that's the first ratoon and you can go on and on, but of course it gets weaker and weaker. So I think they only had one year or maximum two years. In some places, nowadays, in Fiji where there's no control, there are eight or nine times.

Then the cutting was done with a little portable railway which came from the mill, so the mill organized the harvest. So that when the cane came from the land it didn't spend any time waiting around and losing sugar content, it went straight in because they phased it. It was a very efficient organization. I think it was about nine tons of cane to one ton of sugar.

Out there my head was full of lineage and clan structures, the Nuer[68] and so on, but these just didn't fit. The only thing I could do was to look at informal groups because there weren't any formal groups, there were factions which interacted about various things. Trying to measure, I didn't know how to do it numerically, the articulation of the settlement, how news went from one place to another. This is a notional, descriptive thing, but in terms of articulation I came back to see how these were all cut and dried.

AM: Did this lead into your well-known work on quasi-groups.
ACM: Yes. I had an idea of pushing this further because after I had done a village study, which showed that caste was really kinship actually, if you looked at in terms of the internal organization not in terms of the external organization which was paradoxically in the village. The internal organization was in the region, that is the marriage area, and the external was in thc village with the smaller group which you would think would be the other way round wouldn't you?

I did that study in the '50s and then in the '60s I went to the county town, which had been the princely capital where E.M. Forster's[69] 'Maharaja'[70] lived because I reckoned that at that time there were village studies just coming out, and there were studies of cities and so on, but there was nothing about a small market town. At that time the district town totalled 30,000–35,000, now it's 350,000. I saw it as the focus of three interlocking spheres, one was the hierarchy of the local government, where under Nehru's[71] government village councils had been started, then circles of villages made the next tier, then a district elected body of villagers. This was a village hierarchy in which of course some of the villagers were really good politicians, and then interlocking with that was the political party organization which covered the town and the whole district and the third was the municipality where these political parties' leaders fought it out with elections. So, the three spheres interlocked in this district town and I had the idea of writing a book about this, cross-cutting them with the kinds of action sets which were formed drawing from these three spheres and the kinds of factions that existed.

It was a nice idea but I never carried it out because when I got back at the end of 1960–61, Philip Mason[72] at the Institute of Race

Relations asked me to write a book on the history of the Fiji Indians and it seemed to me that that was a very necessary thing to do because they were discriminated against and no one liked them in Fiji, and no one thought they had a history. I wrote that book which took most of the end 1961–62 as I had to go to all the colonial records and so on to really set the record straight and that was published in 1963. By then this district thing was a bit cooler than it had been.

The next year Fürer-Haimendorf[73] who was always avid to get people out into the field because he liked going to the field so much himself, I think, said, 'Go to Pakistan and see the possibilities for fieldwork there', which sounded very interesting. I had six months in Pakistan visiting 10 different districts, finding the sort of things that could be researched. The last week I was there I got a letter inviting me to be the editor of the new *Man*,[74] so I got waylaid. After that I was six years on the SSRC[75] [Social Science Research Council] which took a lot of time, so I never got back to the study of interlocking spheres, but the data are there in the archive, I have the field notes and journal and so on.

AM: To go back to the chronology, you came back from Fiji, then did you get a job?
ACM: No, no. The Australians were kind enough to give me a fellowship on the basis of the Fiji stuff, and that is when I did the Indian village study, it was with Australian money.

AM: Then you wrote that into a book?
ACM: Then I wrote that into a book. I was in Canberra when Nadel died at the beginning of 1956. Haimendorf was building up the department. He had already got Colin Rosser and Freddy Bailey[76] and he asked me if I wanted to come to London and I thought it was probably a good idea.

AM: Tell me something about Christoph because he was my....
ACM: You know more about Christoph than I do.

AM: Possibly.
ACM: He was a very engaging person. As a departmental head, on the one hand he was a very good academic politician. People underestimated him. After all he had been in the Nizam's Government

as an advisor, so you had to look after your interests there I should think. There were quite a few sharks in that outfit I daresay. He was really quite good at keeping the department afloat and expanding the department. On the other hand, I think he was a facilitator; if you wanted to go to the field, he would do his best to get you there or whatever it was. He was never didactic about what should be done, it was left up to you. He had a very light hand in that way.

AM: How do you rate him as an anthropologist or an ethnographer?
ACM: Well, I think the ethnography is a little old-fashioned, I suppose, but is very thorough. The Gond stuff – I have never seen his notebooks but I would have thought he was pretty thorough. I took the book *Notes and Queries*[77] the first time so that I wouldn't miss anything out.

AM: Did you see any of his films?
ACM: Films? I'm not very good at assessing films but he was an explorer. He was one of the explorer-scholars in that line, the opening up of Nepal absolutely suited him fine. He was the first person up into Mustang.[78] He was the first person, I daresay, who knew how to work the aristocracy in Kathmandu and so on. In a way people under-rated him.

AM: He was there when Dor Bahadur Bista[79] came to SOAS as his assistant?
ACM: I don't really remember much about what Dor Bahadur did. But what was he, an informant?

AM: Yes. But he later became a professor of anthropology at Tribhuvan.[80]
ACM: At Tribhuvan, yes.

AM: He later wrote important books about....
ACM: They were good, were they?

AM: Yes.
ACM: I can't remember him giving any papers at SOAS.

AM: He'd hoped to stay on at SOAS and was rather disappointed that Christoph couldn't get him a job there.
ACM: I see.

AM: But what about the others? John Middleton[81] was there?
ACM: Yes. John was there, Phil Gulliver[82] was there. Who else?

AM: Abner Cohen?[83]
ACM: Abner Cohen, yes. Goodness me, because the Department finally got to cover more or less all the fields. Chinese, who was in Chinese? Woody Watson,[84] yes. He went to Harvard.

AM: Yes, that's right.
ACM: I haven't really kept in touch. It's been 30 years now, and the place has changed so much now, it is so large. There may be three times as many students as there were and when I went to SOAS there were hardly any undergraduates at all for my first two or three years. I think they started with Abdullah Bujra and David Parkin. I think all the lecturing was done at the LSE.

AM: Was it?
ACM: I have a feeling, yes. The examining was done with the Examiners Board for three colleges, so we were very late with the undergraduate field.

AM: Who do you think, whether it's anthropologists or anyone most influenced your work? I mean I know you were influenced by those Frenchmen Dumont[85] and co.
ACM: Dumont is hard to be failed. At one time, because I was interested in things like factions and quasi-groups, not formal groups, I suppose then I gravitated down to action sets, the nature of action Parsons[86] coming from Weber.[87]

AM: John Barnes?[88]
ACM: John Barnes, no.

AM: He worked on networks.
ACM: That was later, I think.

AM: Yes, it was.
ACM: Finally, what get on to is rational. What goes on in the black box you can't really tell. Well, I don't think you can.

I then got on to kingship jag. This was another thing which I suppose diverted me from trying to write articles. This was through Forster's 'Maharajah's' son whom I knew for many years, and in

’80 or ’81 we were talking. I interviewed him several times about what kind of a king he thought he was and how he felt about it. He said, ‘Well, you really ought to go around and interview people who still remember those days, and who actually made kings’. He said, ‘If you don’t do it now, they won’t be around’.

In 1982 I spent several months in Maharashtra and Rajasthan, and then later in South India, interviewing all the people who had been involved in either the secular or religious part of making these rulers kings. I interviewed them with tape and then I transcribed it all, then I digitized it, so it’s about 300–400 pages of digitized material. They are quite interesting to read though there is a lot of duplication of course. Then you find when you are in one state or another there are a lot of idiosyncratic ways of interpreting things, so that it is actually more interesting than I thought it might be.

I couldn’t keep all the tapes because I was travelling round with a bedding roll, so I transcribed them in the evening. The English ones I transcribed literally, those in Hindi I translated as I went along, so an approximation but I wasn’t doing textual analysis. In some ways it is not academic because it’s not fieldwork because there you can go back and check, whereas here I would leave one place and go on to another, so I learnt some more in place B but couldn’t go back to place A and see if that applied there, it was better than nothing.

AM: You mention several times Forster’s ‘Maharaja’. I think you met Forster on occasion.

ACM: Yes. But this is a short talk. This was before I went to the village that I have been interested in which was in Forster’s ‘Maharajah’s’ state, I went to see Forster. I don’t think he had much to say because he hadn’t been to many villages. As I said to you, the only thing I remember was that I used the word viable, which he picked up as a neologism which he didn’t approve of. I took part twice in the ritual Birth of Krishna[89] which is the climax to the *Passage to India*[90] ritual, which he must talk about in the *Hill of Devi* sometime, and that was great fun. You played around as Krishna as a baby and went to the palace for eight days and sang hymns in honour of Krishna, you were there at the birth, you took Krishna through the town and put him in the lake, more or less as

Forster describes it. In those days, this was in the '50s, there was enough of the old Dewas army, the camels were still there and the elephants were still there, to make quite a nice procession as it went through this little town. I enjoyed that. Then after the procession His Highness would invite us to have a peg or two and unwind.

AM: We're just about coming to an end, but is there any thing you would've liked me to ask you about, obviously...were missed out. But is there anything particular that I should've mentioned, your family? Or your wife, or your...?

ACM: My wife came. She was in the field with me. She was a painter, an artist, etching and so on. She had a good life doing that. She came on the tour of all these princely states. We enjoyed that.

AM: Did you take Swan Hellenic?[91]

ACM: I am a believer in the Hindu idea of the four stages of life.[92] And it was quite clear, I had my stage as a student as an ascetic, a celibate student, until I finished my time with the ambulance unit. I was then working in India and I was of course celibate.

Then when I got back to England, I got married in 1949 and I started the *grihastha ashrama*[93] (householder) stage, got both my daughters married off, so I did all my paternal duties, and that ended on 30 September 1985 when my time in SOAS came to an end. After that, you are supposed to go to the forest and start thinking deep thoughts. I didn't do that but I didn't keep on professionally. I had things to finish in the anthropological field like some work on Japanese imperial work. But then I took on lecture tours. First, I was lecturing with Swan Hellenic and then I made my own tours, which were 'off piste' you might say, because there are many, many places, there are hundreds of places in India that people who have seen the other places would like to see.

Take Benares, everyone goes to Benares on all the tours, but if you go 30–40 miles north-west you get to Jaunpur. And Jaunpur, after Timur[94] sacked Delhi, all the craftsmen left and were refugees and the ruler of Jaunpur suddenly found himself without an overlord, got these people in, and he made two or three mosques in a style which is found nowhere else, they have great slanting pylons in the front, very magnificent buildings. There is also a Mughal bridge in Jaunpur with places for the shops on it, it's not far.

If you go the other way along the Grand Trunk Road you only go 50 miles and you get to Sasaram where Sher Shah[95] has his mausoleum, his father first and then him. His father has the Sukha Rauza, the dry mausoleum, and Sher Shah who was the ruler before the Mughals, has the wet mausoleum. It is in the middle of a lake and is a beautiful place. To my mind of the three most beautiful mausolea the first is the Taj, and the second the mausoleum of Rukn-i-'Alam in Multan, but the third is definitely Sher Shah's in Sasaram, and no one goes there.

It is these sorts of places which I took people to and it was the greatest fun, and I saw hundreds of places which I never would have gone to. So, you have a feeling of the country as a whole. The first time I had that feeling really I suppose was in 1945–46 when I was in the ambulance unit when I went to Cape Comorin, Kanyakumari, it was in Travancore state,[96] it wasn't in British India at the time; there was simply a headland, no high cliffs, and there was a very old Chola[97] temple, and there were a few rocks, a kind of shoal about half a mile off the sea, and then the Antarctic. There were two buildings there, the Maharaja had a guest house and there was a traveller's bungalow, that was all there was. It was a magic place and standing there one felt the whole weight of this enormous subcontinent bearing down on this tiny point, a very strange feeling.

I have only felt it once before and that was when I was in Argentina and went over to Brazil because there are some famous waterfalls called the Iguazu waterfalls, and you go to the Brazilian side to see another aspect of them and that is right at the bottom south-east corner of Brazil. As I stood there, I felt the whole of Brazil bearing down on this tiny little spot, the Amazon and the Pampas[98] and all the rest of it, a strange feeling.

Now Cape Comorin is a Coney Island, it's a Clacton-on-Sea,[99] everyone goes, foreigners don't go very much because it's not on the route, but the villagers go if they are making a tour of India, because it is fairly near a place called Rameshwaram[100] which is one of the other major temples. You get people selling sea shells and god knows what not. I met people there, because you all go there and see the sun sinking into the sea, the sunset. And there were people in front of me, there were peasants with saffron turbans and wives had the *ghagra*,[101] the big skirts, looking exactly the same as the people in central India that I knew. And I went up to them and said, 'brother, where have you come from?' He came from the next district. I said, 'What community are you?' They said they were Khatis.[102] So I said, 'Oh I know some Khatis, what village are you from?' Extraordinary. My people had married into his village and where we were sitting we were 100 miles away. It could have been Benares, of course, it could have been Haridwar. At these places you get a conflation of villagers, because nowadays villagers go around India. They hire a bus and off they go.

AM: You mentioned four stages. The Hellenic tours were the third. What is the fourth?

ACM: The fourth one is now I am downsizing from a house that I have lived in for 60 years which is quite large and full of detritus from that period, and I am going into a three-room flat. So, there will be a lot of detachment from things which I've grown used to living with. I won't become a hermit but I will be more detached in many ways, in a way I have not been up till now.

AM: Thank you very much and may I wish you all success in your detachment!

NOTES

1. School of Oriental and African Studies (SOAS). 2020. https://bit.ly/33CIzxE

2. The withdrawal of the United Kingdom from the European Union.

3. Johannes Brahms, see Appendix.

4. The Middlesex Regiment (Duke of Cambridge's Own) was a line infantry regiment of the British Army in existence from 1881 until 1966. The regiment was formed, as the Duke of Cambridge's Own (Middlesex Regiment), in 1881 as part of the Childers Reforms when the 57th (West Middlesex) and 77th (East Middlesex) Regiments of Foot were amalgamated with the county's militia and rifle volunteer units. https://en.wikipedia.org/wiki/Middlesex_Regiment

5. North Weald is a village in the civil parish of North Weald Bassett in the Epping Forest district of Essex, England. The village is within the North Weald Ridges and Valleys landscape area. https://en.wikipedia.org/wiki/North_Weald

6. Carl Rosa founded the company in 1873 after several successful years in America as the Parepa-Rosa English Opera Company. The first British performance, Wallace's Maritana, was given on September 1st 1873 at the Theatre Royal, Manchester. For 85 years the Company toured continuously to all the major towns and cities in Great Britain and Ireland and people will always associate opera with the name Carl Rosa. http://www.carlrosaopera.co.uk/history/opera-company.asp

7. Artur Schnabel, see Appendix.

8. Robert Mayer, see Appendix.

9. Harold Sargent, see Appendix.

10. Mozart, see Appendix.

11. A follower of Tolstoy, who advocates and practices manual labour, simplicity of living, non-resistance, etc., holds that possession of wealth and ownership of property are sinful, and rejects all religious teachings not coming directly from Christ. https://en.wiktionary.org/wiki/Tolstoyan

12. A suffragette was a member of an activist women's organizations in the early 20th century who, under the banner 'Votes for Women', fought for the right to vote in public elections, known as women's suffrage. The term refers in particular to members of the British Women's Social and Political Union (WSPU), a women-only movement founded in 1903 by Emmeline Pankhurst, which engaged in direct action and civil disobedience. In 1906, a reporter writing in the *Daily Mail* coined the term suffragette for the WSPU, from suffragist, to belittle the women advocating women's suffrage. The militants embraced the new name, even adopting it for use as the title of the newspaper published by the WSPU. https://en.wikipedia.org/wiki/Suffragette

13. The Irish Renaissance of the late 19th and early 20th century saw a revival of Irish arts and culture influenced by prominent intellectuals like W.B. Yeats, Lady Augusta Gregory, AE, J.M. Synge and Katharine Tynan. https://libraries.indiana.edu/poetry-and-politics-irish-renaissance-and-quest-irish-independence

14. J.M. Synge, see Appendix.

15. Jack Butler Yeats, see Appendix.

16. William Butler Yeats, see Appendix.

17. Maud Gonne MacBride (1866–1953) was an English-born Irish republican revolutionary, suffragette and actress. Of Anglo-Irish descent,

she was won over to Irish nationalism by the plight of evicted people in the Land Wars. She also actively agitated for Home Rule. https://en.wikipedia.org/wiki/Maud_Gonne

18. The 1926 General Strike in the United Kingdom was a general strike that lasted nine days, from 4 to 12 May 1926. It was called by the General Council of the Trades Union Congress (TUC) in an unsuccessful attempt to force the British government to act to prevent wage reductions and worsening conditions for 1.2 million locked-out coal miners. Some 1.7 million workers went out, especially in transport and heavy industry. The government was prepared, and enlisted middle class volunteers to maintain essential services. There was little violence and the TUC gave up in defeat. https://en.wikipedia.org/wiki/1926_United_Kingdom_general_strike

19. Thomas Tilling Ltd, later known with its subsidiary companies as the Tilling Group, was one of two conglomerates that controlled almost all of the major bus operators in the United Kingdom between World Wars I and II and until nationalisation in 1948. Tilling, together with the other conglomerate, British Electric Traction (BET), became the main constituents of the country's nationalised bus industry in the late 1960s and was sufficiently well known to have entered popular culture as part of London's Cockney rhyming slang (Thomas Tilling = shilling). https://en.wikipedia.org/wiki/Thomas_Tilling

20. The Dalton Plan is an educational concept created by Helen Parkhurst. It is inspired by the intellectual ferment at the turn of the 20th century. Educational thinkers such as Maria Montessori and John Dewey influenced Parkhurst while she created the Dalton Plan. Their aim was to achieve a balance between a child's talent and the needs of the community. The Dalton Plan is a method of education by which pupils work at their own pace, and receive individual help from the teacher when necessary. There is no formal class instruction. Students draw up time-tables and are responsible for finishing the work on their syllabuses or assignments. Students are also encouraged to help each other with their work. The underlying aim of the Dalton Plan is to achieve the highest mental, moral, physical and spiritual development of the pupil. https://en.wikipedia.org/wiki/Dalton_Plan

21. Birchington-on-Sea is a village in northeast Kent, England. It is part of the Thanet district and forms part of the civil parish of Birchington. It lies on the coast facing the North Sea, east of the Thames Estuary, between the seaside resorts of Herne Bay and Margate. As a seaside resort, the village is a tourist and retirement destination. The village's Minnis Bay is a family beach with attractions such as sailing, windsurfing, a paddling pool and

coastal walking routes. Its three smaller beaches are surrounded by chalk cliffs, cliff stacks and caves. The village was first recorded in 1240. https://en.wikipedia.org/wiki/Birchington-on-Sea

22. Littlehampton is a town, seaside resort and pleasure harbour, and the most populous civil parish in West Sussex, England. It lies on the English Channel. https://en.wikipedia.org/wiki/Littlehampton

23. Bryanston School is a co-educational independent school for day and boarding pupils, located next to the village of Bryanston, and near the town of Blandford Forum, in Dorset in South West England. It was founded in 1928. It occupies a palatial country house designed and built in 1889–94 by Richard Norman Shaw, the champion of a renewed academic tradition, for Viscount Portman, the owner of large tracts in the West End of London, in the early version of neo-Georgian style that Sir Edwin Lutyens called 'Wrenaissance', to replace an earlier house, and is set in 400 acres (1.6 km^2). Bryanston is a member of the Headmasters' and Headmistresses' Conference and the Eton Group. It has a reputation as a liberal and artistic school using some ideas of the Dalton Plan. https://en.wikipedia.org/wiki/Bryanston_School

24. Thorold Francis Coade (1896–1963) was a British school teacher and headmaster. Coade was headmaster at Bryanston School in Dorset for much of his career (1932–59), succeeding J.G. Jeffreys. He believed in self-discipline and developed this ethos at the school. He developed 'pioneering' at the school to augment sports, consisting of community-related activities, such as forestry in the extensive grounds of the school. Coade was keen on drama and the school's theatre is named the Coade Hall in his memory. https://en.wikipedia.org/wiki/Thorold_Coade

25. Michael Howard, see Appendix.

26. Cavalaire-sur-Mer is a commune in the Var department in the Provence-Alpes-Côte d'Azur region in south-eastern France. The name is probably derived from an ancient Phoenician colony of the name of Heracles Caccabaria. There are also remains of a Gallo-Roman occupation in Pardigon. The town was detached from Gassin in 1929. https://en.wikipedia.org/wiki/Cavalaire-sur-Mer

27. In 2015 the first Dorchester Cider Festival & Perry in The Park took place at the beautiful Borough Gardens. Roughly 15 cider producers typically attend the festival's cider village. Together they offer over 80 different types of cider to sample. Ranging from traditional scrumpy for the purists to raspberry and bubble gum flavours – ensuring there is everything under the sun to choose from. The food village also offers a wide variety

of locally produced dishes to try. https://dorchesterroundtable.co.uk/dorchester-cider-festival/

28. The first exam taken at university towards a BA degree, discontinued during the 20th century.

29. Euclid, see Appendix.

30. Nikolay Lobachevsky, see Appendix.

31. In liberal arts education, the quadrivium consists of the four subjects or arts (namely arithmetic, geometry, music, and astronomy) taught after teaching the trivium. The word is Latin, meaning four ways, and its use for the four subjects has been attributed to Boethius or Cassiodorus in the 6th century. Together, the trivium and the quadrivium comprised the seven liberal arts (based on thinking skills) as distinguished from the practical arts (such as medicine and architecture); The trivium is the lower division of the seven liberal arts and comprises grammar, logic, and rhetoric. https://en.wikipedia.org/wiki/Quadrivium & https://en.wikipedia.org/wiki/Trivium

32. Members of the Religious Society of Friends, a Christian movement founded by George Fox c. 1650 and devoted to peaceful principles. Central to the Quakers' belief is the doctrine of the 'Inner Light', or sense of Christ's direct working in the soul. This has led them to reject both formal ministry and all set forms of worship.

33. Unitarianism (from Latin unitas 'unity, oneness', from unus 'one') is a Christian theological movement named for its belief that the God in Christianity is one person, as opposed to the Trinity (tri-from Latin tres 'three') which in most other branches of Christianity defines God as one being in three persons: the Father, Son, and Holy Spirit. Unitarian Christians, therefore, believe that Jesus was inspired by God in his moral teachings, and he is a saviour, but he was not a deity or God incarnate. https://en.wikipedia.org/wiki/Unitarianism

34. The Friends' Ambulance Unit (FAU) was a volunteer ambulance service, founded by individual members of the British Religious Society of Friends (Quakers), in line with their Peace Testimony. The FAU operated from 1914–19, 1939–46 and 1946–59 in 25 different countries around the world. It was independent of the Quakers' organisation and chiefly staffed by registered conscientious objectors. https://rb.gy/0oq3ts

35. The Royal Army Medical Corps (RAMC) is a specialist corps in the British Army which provides medical services to all Army personnel and their families, in war and in peace. Medical services in the British armed services date from the formation of the Standing Regular Army after the Restoration

of Charles II in 1660. This was the first time a career was provided for a Medical Officer (MO), both in peacetime and in war. https://en.wikipedia.org/wiki/Royal_Army_Medical_Corps

36. The Normandy landings were the landing operations and associated airborne operations on Tuesday, 6 June 1944 of the Allied invasion of Normandy in Operation Overlord during World War II. Codenamed Operation Neptune and often referred to as D-Day, it was the largest seaborne invasion in history. The operation began the liberation of German-occupied France (and later western Europe) and laid the foundations of the Allied victory on the Western Front. https://en.wikipedia.org/wiki/Normandy_landings

37. Hexylresorcinol is an organic compound with local anaesthetic, antiseptic, and anthelmintic properties. https://en.wikipedia.org/wiki/Hexylresorcinol

38. The Madras Presidency, or the Presidency of Fort St. George, and also known as Madras Province, was an administrative subdivision (presidency) of British India. At its greatest extent, the presidency included most of southern India, including the whole of the Indian state of Andhra Pradesh, and parts of Tamil Nadu, Kerala, Karnataka, Telangana, Odisha and the union territory of Lakshadweep. The city of Madras was the winter capital of the Presidency and Ootacamund or Ooty, the summer capital. The Island of Ceylon was a part of Madras Presidency from 1793 to 1798 when it was created a Crown colony. https://en.wikipedia.org/wiki/Madras_Presidency

39. In India, Pakistan, and Bangladesh, a tehsildar is a tax officer accompanied by revenue inspectors. They are in charge of obtaining taxes from a tehsil with regard to land revenue. https://en.wikipedia.org/wiki/Tehsildar

40. Xiamen Island, alternately known as Amoy Island from its Hokkien pronunciation, is an island in southeastern Fujian, China, on the Taiwan Strait. It is administered by the People's Republic of China as the Huli and Siming urban districts of the sub-provincial city of Xiamen. https://en.wikipedia.org/wiki/Xiamen_Island

41. The Kuomintang (KMT) often referred to in English as the Nationalist Party or Chinese Nationalist Party (CNP), is a major political party in Taiwan (Republic of China) based in Taipei. Formed in 1919, the KMT was the sole ruling party of the Republic of China from 1928 to 2000 and is currently an opposition political party in the Legislative Yuan. https://en.wikipedia.org/wiki/Kuomintang

42. Tianjin alternately Tientsin, is a municipality and a coastal metropolis in Northern China on the shore of the Bohai Sea. It is one of the nine national central cities in Mainland China. https://en.wikipedia.org/wiki/Tianjin

43. The Temple of Heaven is an imperial complex of religious buildings situated in the south-eastern part of central Beijing. The complex was visited by the Emperors of the Ming and Qing dynasties for annual ceremonies of prayer to Heaven for a good harvest. https://en.wikipedia.org/wiki/Temple_of_Heaven

44. The Forbidden City is a palace complex in central Beijing, China. It houses the Palace Museum, and was the former Chinese imperial palace and state residence of the Emperor of China from the Ming dynasty (since the Yongle Emperor) to the end of the Qing dynasty, between 1420 and 1924. The Forbidden City served as the home of Chinese emperors and their households and was the ceremonial and political centre of the Chinese government for almost 500 years. https://en.wikipedia.org/wiki/Forbidden_City

45. The Drum Tower of Beijing, or Gulou is situated at the northern end of the central axis of the Inner City to the north of Di'anmen Street. Originally built for musical reasons, it was later used to announce the time and is now a tourist attraction. https://rb.gy/vaaf9f

46. The Burma Road was a road linking Burma with the southwest of China. Its terminals were Kunming, Yunnan, and Lashio, Burma. It was built while Burma was a British colony to convey supplies to China during the Second Sino-Japanese War. Preventing the flow of supplies on the road helped motivate the occupation of Burma by the Empire of Japan in 1942. Use of the road was restored to the Allies in 1945 after the completion of the Ledo Road. Some parts of the old road are still visible today. https://en.wikipedia.org/wiki/Burma_Road

47. Suzhou alternately Soochow is a major city located in south-eastern Jiangsu Province of East China. https://en.wikipedia.org/wiki/Suzhou

48. Yan'an is a prefecture-level city in the Shanbei region of Shaanxi province, China, bordering Shanxi to the east and Gansu to the west. It administers several counties, including Zhidan (formerly Bao'an), which served as the headquarters of the Chinese Communists before the city of Yan'an proper took that role. https://rb.gy/tpclhj

49. The *dhoti* is fashioned out of a rectangular piece of unstitched cloth, usually around 4.5 metres (15 ft) long, wrapped around the waist and the legs and knotted either in the front or the back; The *lungi* is a type of sarong that originated in the Indian subcontinent, it is a traditional skirt-like

lower garment wrapped around the waist, usually below the belly. https://en.wikipedia.org/wiki/Dhoti & https://en.wikipedia.org/wiki/Lungi

50. *Mantou* often referred to as Chinese steamed bun, is a white and soft type of steamed bread or bun popular in Northern China. https://en.wikipedia.org/wiki/Mantou

51. Cyril Belshaw, see Appendix.

52. Founded in 1916 as the School of Oriental Studies, it took its present title in 1938, by which time it had also established itself as a centre for African Studies. It moved to its present site in 1941. https://www.soas.ac.uk/about/history/

53. Raymond Firth, see Appendix.

54. Bronisław Malinowski, see Appendix.

55. Siegfried Nadel, see Appendix.

56. Edmund Leach, see Appendix.

57. Audrey Richards, see Appendix.

58. Isaac Schapera, see Appendix.

59. Herbert Hogbin, see Appendix.

60. John Hutton, see Appendix.

61. A goatee is a style of facial hair incorporating hair on one's chin but not on one's cheeks. The exact nature of the style has varied according to time and culture.

62. The Laccadive Islands or Cannanore Islands are one of the three island subgroups in the Union Territory of Lakshadweep, India. It is the central subgroup of the Lakshadweep, separated from the Amindivi Islands subgroup roughly by the 11th parallel north and from the atoll of Minicoy (Maliku) – far to the south – by the 9 Degree or Mamala Channel. https://en.wikipedia.org/wiki/Laccadive_Islands

63. The Trobriand Islands are a 450-square-kilometre (174-square-mile) archipelago of coral atolls off the east coast of New Guinea. They are part of the nation of Papua New Guinea and are in Milne Bay Province. https://en.wikipedia.org/wiki/Trobriand_Islands

64. The Australian National University (ANU) is a national research university located in Canberra, the capital of Australia. Its main campus in Acton encompasses seven teaching and research colleges, in addition to several national academies and institutes. Established in 1946, ANU is the only university to have been created by the Parliament of Australia. It traces its origins to Canberra University College, which was established in 1929 and was integrated into ANU in 1960. https://en.wikipedia.org/wiki/Australian_National_University

65. Douglas Copland, see Appendix.

66. Chief.

67. A new shoot or sprout springing from the base of a crop plant, especially sugar cane, after cropping.

68. The Nuer people are a Nilotic ethnic group concentrated in the Greater Upper Nile region of South Sudan and are from Ethiopia's Gambela Region. They speak the Nuer language, which belongs to the Nilotic language family. They are the second largest ethnic group in south Sudan and the second major ethnic group in Gambella. The Nuer people are pastoralists who herd cattle for a living. https://en.wikipedia.org/wiki/Nuer_people

69. E.M. Forster, see Appendix.

70. The *Hill of Devi* is an account by E.M. Forster of two visits to India in 1912–13 and 1921, during which he worked as the private secretary to Tukojirao III, the Maharaja of the state of Dewas Senior. https://en.wikipedia.org/wiki/The_Hill_of_Devi

71. Jawaharlal Nehru, see Appendix.

72. Philip Mason, see Appendix.

73. Christoph von Fürer-Haimendorf, see Appendix.

74. The *Journal of the Royal Anthropological Institute*, formerly *Man*, was established in 1901 and is a quarterly journal with articles on all aspects of anthropology, as well as correspondence and a section of book reviews. https://bit.ly/3iBHgDb

75. The Social Science Research Council (SSRC) is a US-based independent, international non-profit organization dedicated to advancing research in the social sciences and related disciplines. Established in Manhattan in 1923, it today maintains a headquarters in Brooklyn Heights with a staff of approximately 70, and small regional offices in other parts of the world. The SSRC offers several fellowships to researchers in the social sciences and related disciplines, including for international fieldwork. https://en.wikipedia.org/wiki/Social_Science_Research_Council

76. Frederick Bailey, see Appendix.

77. *Notes and Queries on Anthropology* was published by the British Association for the Advancement of Science and edited by John George Garson and Charles Hercules Read. The first edition was published in 1874. https://s.si.edu/30KCMUP

78. Mustang district is one of the 77 districts of Nepal. The headquarters is Jomsom. The district is in Dhawalagiri Zone and part of Gandaki Pradesh in northern Nepal, straddles the Himalayas and extends northward onto the Tibetan Plateau. The district is one of the remotest areas in Nepal and

is second in terms of the sparsity of population. The elevation ranges from 1,372 to 8,167 meters, Mount Dhaulagiri, the 7th highest mountain in the world, with several peaks above 7,000 meters. https://en.wikipedia.org/wiki/Mustang_District

79. Dor Bahadur Bista (born c. 1924–26) is a Nepalese anthropologist, social scientist and activist. Bista is considered the father of Nepalese anthropology, and has published such popular books as *Fatalism and Development: Nepal's Struggle for Modernization* and *People of Nepal.* Bista mysteriously disappeared in 1995. https://en.wikipedia.org/wiki/Dor_Bahadur_Bista

80. Tribhuvan University (TU), established in 1959, is the first national institution of higher education in Nepal. http://www.tribhuvan-university.edu.np/

81. John Middleton, see Appendix.

82. Philip Gulliver, see Appendix.

83. Abner Cohen, see Appendix.

84. James Watson, see Appendix.

85. Louis Dumont, see Appendix.

86. Talcott Parsons, see Appendix.

87. Max Weber, see Appendix.

88. John Arundel Barnes, see Appendix.

89. Krishna Janmashtami, also known simply as Janmashtami or Gokulashtami, is an annual Hindu festival that celebrates the birth of Krishna, the eighth avatar of Vishnu. It is observed according to the Hindu lunisolar calendar, on the eighth day (*Ashtami*) of the *Krishna Paksha* (dark fortnight) in *Shraavana* or *Bhadrapad* (depending on whether the calendar chooses the new moon or full moon day as the last day of the month), which overlaps with August or September of the Gregorian calendar. https://en.wikipedia.org/wiki/Krishna_Janmashtami

90. *A Passage to India* (1924) is a novel by English author E.M. Forster set against the backdrop of the British Raj and the Indian independence movement in the 1920s. It was selected as one of the 100 great works of 20th century English literature by the Modern Library and won the 1924 James Tait Black Memorial Prize for fiction. https://en.wikipedia.org/wiki/A_Passage_to_India

91. Swan Hellenic is a British cruise line specialising in expedition tours of historical or cultural interest aimed at the upper end of the cruise market. Swan Hellenic was first established as Swan's Tours in the 1950s as a tour operator carrying guests to historic sites, providing enrichment throughout their trips. https://en.wikipedia.org/wiki/Swan_Hellenic

92. Hindu philosophy traditionally observes four stages of life. These stages are known as *ashramas*. *Brahmacharya* is the first stage of life. It is the student stage of life, preparing for success in later stages of life. The second stage is called *Grihastha*. Known as the 'householder' stage, it follows what most people do naturally after leaving school: Maintaining a home, having a family. *Vanaprashta* is the third stage. It begins after individuals fulfil their obligations to their families. The fourth stage is *Sannyasa*, renunciation. There are two traditional entry points into this stage of life. https://www.hinduamerican.org/blog/what-are-the-four-stages-of-hindu-life/

93. See Appendix, Philip Hugh Gulliver.

94. Timur (1336–1405) later Tim⊠r Gurk⊠n⊠ sometimes spelled Taimur and historically best known as Amir Timur or Tamerlane was a Turco-Mongol conqueror who founded the Timurid Empire in and around modern-day Afghanistan, Iran and Central Asia, becoming the first ruler of the Timurid dynasty. https://en.wikipedia.org/wiki/Timur

95. Sher Shah Suri (1486–1545) born Far⊠d Kh⊠n, was the founder of the Suri Empire in India, with its capital in Sasaram in modern-day Bihar. https://en.wikipedia.org/wiki/Sher_Shah_Suri

96. Kanyakumari (also known as Cape Comorin) is a town in Kanyakumari District in the state of Tamil Nadu in India. The southernmost town in mainland India, it is sometimes referred to as 'the Land's End'; The Kingdom of Travancore was an Indian kingdom from c. 870 until 1949. It was ruled by the Travancore Royal Family from Padmanabhapuram, and later Thiruvananthapuram. At its zenith, the kingdom covered most of modern-day central and southern Kerala with the Thachudaya Kaimal's enclave of Irinjalakuda Koodalmanikyam temple in the neighbouring Kingdom of Cochin, as well as the district of Kanyakumari, now in the Indian state of Tamil Nadu. https://en.wikipedia.org/wiki/Kanyakumari & https://en.wikipedia.org/wiki/Travancore

97. The Chola dynasty was a Tamil thalassocratic empire of southern India, one of the longest-ruling dynasties in the world's history. The earliest datable references to the Chola are in inscriptions from the 3rd century BCE left by Ashoka, of the Maurya Empire (Ashoka Major Rock Edict No. 13). https://en.wikipedia.org/wiki/Chola_dynasty

98. The Pampas (from the Quechua: pampa, meaning 'plain') are fertile South American lowlands that cover more than 1,200,000 km^2 and include the Argentine provinces of Buenos Aires, La Pampa, Santa Fe, Entre Ríos and Córdoba; all of Uruguay; and Brazil's southernmost state, Rio Grande do Sul. https://rb.gy/ptiiqm

99. Clacton-on-Sea is the largest town in the Tendring peninsula and district in Essex, eastern England, and was founded as an urban district in 1871. It is a seaside resort that saw a peak of tourists in the summer months between the 1950s and 1970s. https://en.wikipedia.org/wiki/Clacton-on-Sea

100. Rameswaram (also spelt as Ramesvaram, Rameshwaram) is a town and municipality in the Ramanathapuram district of the Indian state of Tamil Nadu. It is on Pamban Island separated from mainland India by the Pamban channel and is about 40 kilometres from Mannar Island, Sri Lanka. https://en.wikipedia.org/wiki/Rameswaram

101. A long full skirt, often decorated with embroidery, mirrors, or bells worn in South Asia.

102. Khati is an Indian caste. Its members live mainly in and around the Malwa region. Its main language is Malwi. https://en.wikipedia.org/wiki/Khati

PART two

M.N. Srinivas. Photograph courtesy Alan Macfarlane.

M.N. Srinivas

Mysore Narasimhachar Srinivas *(16 November 1916 – 30 November 1999) has been one of India's most distinguished sociologists and social anthropologists. His contribution to the disciplines of sociology and social anthropology and to public life in India was unique. He was an institution builder, a creative researcher and a devoted teacher, combining all of his roles in a remarkable way.*

He received honours from the University of Bombay, the Royal Anthropological Institute, and the Government of France. In 1977, he was awarded the Padma Bhushan. He was the honorary foreign member of two prestigious academies: the British Academy and the American Academy of Arts and Sciences.

His work The Remembered Village *(1976) is considered a classic. It is a study based on the 11 months he spent in the village in 1948 and on subsequent visits until 1964. His other prominent works were* Religion and Society among the Coorgs of South India *(1952),* Caste in Modern India and Other Essays *(1962),* Social Change in Modern India *(1966) and* Marriage and Family in Mysore *(1942).*[1]

Jack Goody (JG): We are pleased to have Professor Srinivas with us this afternoon. He came to Cambridge from the University of Mysore[2] for this term, to give the Fraser Lecture, and we thought we would take the opportunity of his presence here, of getting him to talk a little about his own career in social anthropology, both in relationship to the people he met, and in relationship to the problems with which he himself dealt, and particularly, perhaps, saying how much social anthropology had changed, or not changed, in India, during the years he had been associated with it.

I first met Professor Srinivas at Oxford in the distant past, but before that, he had been a student at Bombay, so perhaps I might ask you to begin in that ambience.

M.N. Srinivas (MNS): I went to Bombay in the '30s, from Mysore, because my teachers in Mysore had advised me that the best sociologist in India was then teaching in Bombay, and he was Ghurye.[3] And Ghurye, incidentally, was perhaps one of the last students of Rivers[4] in Cambridge.

I went to Ghurye, very raw and immature, and perhaps an opinionated young man. And I told Ghurye, I think, that I wanted to write two volumes on Indian sociology. He smiled and said, 'You will do that', and then, he asked me to do a dissertation on marriage and family among the Kannada castes in Mysore. I think he found me too much out of touch with facts, and he wanted to teach me some respect for facts. I did this dissertation largely out of gazetteers and volumes on tribes and castes, eked out with some fieldwork. And the fieldwork portion was quite interesting, it was even exciting as I remember now.

I got my Masters, and then I proceeded to do a PhD on the Coorgs[5] of South India with Ghurye. This was a thesis based on fieldwork. Coorg in those days – this was during World War II – in

This interview was conducted by Jack Goody, Stephen Levinson and Alan Macfarlane on 24 September 1982. The transcription for this interview was provided by Meenakshi Jauhari Chawla, for this volume.
These interviews are available for viewing on:
https://www.sms.cam.ac.uk/media/1130578
https://www.youtube.com/watch?v=QyR1DW1-gAA

those days, was still somewhat cut off. We had buses from Mysore to the capital Markera[6] and beyond, but Coorg was quite a wild country in those days, with very few restaurants or hotels. And I had to stay in the homes of friends to do my fieldwork. And as it happened, I came down with some very severe stomach trouble, and this destroyed any notions I had of staying in a Coorg village and seeing everything for myself. So, after I had been treated for my stomach trouble, I used to pay visits to Markera and from there, go to the interior, witness ceremonies and visit temples, talk to people. And this was how the material was gathered. I spent several weeks in Markera and I was lucky enough to come across a very learned and also very well-informed Coorg, who taught me about the language, the customs, beliefs etc. and he also helped me translate some of the Coorg folklore I had collected.

And the result of my efforts was a somewhat heavy thesis – about 900 pages, if I remember rightly. And I submitted it to the University of Bombay in 1944. And I think I didn't collect my degree. I got it in '45.

And from Bombay I came to Oxford, on the recommendation of Ghurye, who told me that, unlike Malinowski,[7] Radcliffe-Brown[8] was a seeded functionalist, and it is interesting, because Radcliffe-Brown was, I think, the first student of Rivers at Cambridge.

I came to Oxford in May 1945. Radcliffe-Brown had returned a few months previously from a rather extended stay in São Paulo in Brazil. And the subject of my PhD dissertation was not approved by him. I had chosen as the subject of my dissertation, an examination of the concept of patterns of culture by Ruth Benedict,[9] taking material from three South Indian tribes or marginal groups: two of them being Todas[10] and Chenchus,[11] I'm not sure about the second and the third one being of course, Coorgs.

Radcliffe-Brown did not like Ruth Benedict's approach, thought her highly unscientific, but I wanted to stick up for my choice of theme. I think he was very patient with me, and before he went for the summer vacation, he said, 'If you want to do... if you want to work on patterns of culture, write me a long paper on it during the long vacation, and then we shall decide, during the coming

Michaelmas term'.[12] I worked quite hard during that summer vacation and produced a paper of sorts, and I gave it to Radcliffe-Brown to read. A few days afterwards, he returned the paper to me, and said, 'It's alright you can go on and work on patterns of culture. I'd won my point, but I could see that he was not very happy about it'.

I then asked him, 'Look, what exactly do you think about my theme? Do you think it's useful for me to work on it now that I've been given the permission by you to work on it? What do you think of it?' He said that, I remember the words, 'It's a waste of time for a man of your talents to spend any time on Ruth Benedict!'

I said, 'What shall I do then?' And I had not forgotten the fact that I had burned the poor man with these two volumes of mine to take home with him to Wales for the summer vacation. He said, 'I've just been looking at your Coorg thesis. Did you go to any English school?' I said, 'No, I went to a neighbourhood school'. Then he said something very highly complimentary about my written English, and said, 'There is wonderful material here; why don't you look at this material from the functionalist point of view?' I said, 'Look, I do not have the funds to make another field trip to Coorg – it will be very expensive and it's beyond my means'. He said, 'You needn't go to Coorg, there's plenty of material here. Why don't you look at it? You can register yourself for a PhD'.

So, I registered myself for a PhD with the title, 'The social function of religion in a South Indian community'. And that was how the Coorg book came to be written. Radcliffe-Brown insisted that I read, very rightly, Fustel de Coulanges.[13] He was a great admirer of Fustel de Coulanges, what's that book…?

JG: *The Ancient City*?[14]

MNS: *The Ancient City.* Durkheim[15] and Bateson[16] and then, of course, Evans-Pritchard's[17] Azande volume and *The Nuer*. I read, of course, of his own writings, *The Andaman Islanders*,[18] and so on. I really worked hard. I looked at my data from the functionalist point of view. And suddenly it started falling in place.

I might add here that Ghurye was still committed to Rivers' ideas in his last phase. I think, Rivers, in 1922, had formed a kind of triumvirate with Perry[19] and Elliot Smith,[20] and they have a diffusionism of a very wild sort, saying that human creativity is limited, and some of the best ideas did occur in ancient Egypt, and then they travelled to the rest of the world. I wrote my Coorg book under this unfortunate theoretical framework, if I may call it that. I discovered, or rather, I was extremely dissatisfied with the result of my efforts. Ultimately it came to: where did the Coorgs come from? Some people had brought them in from the Gulf countries, as they are called now, some others had brought them in from Central Asia. The Coorgs themselves knew about both these hypotheses. One knowledgeable Coorg would favour the Gulf states, another Central Asia, you see. I think, both of them based on an equal measure of ignorance. I looked for some physical anthropological data, and all that I know about them is that they have extreme black syphilis[21] amongst them, you see, and this, I think, posed a problem to the people who swore that they were Aryans.[22]

And I turned to Haddon's[23] *Races of Man*,[24] I think there's a book called that. I found Haddon had introduced a second migration of Aryans in the second edition of his *Races of Man* without informing that it was a new edition, you see. I'm mentioning all this because this kind of diffusionism was a guessing game, and I was fed up with it, you see. I told myself I'll go to Oxford and if I can't get to a sociology which is more definitive, then I'm going to quit the field and do something else.

And Radcliffe-Brown's functionalism was extremely helpful, and looking at the good material from a Durkheimian[25] and Radcliffe-Brown point of view, I found, it made a lot of sense to me. At last I had come to a sociology which was, on the one hand, related to empirical data. On the other hand, it produced some theoretical insights into Indian culture and society. I felt I had come home.

And this is why I feel that, you know, nowadays Radcliffe-Brown's reputation is not very high, particularly in England. I think people do not know the kind of importance his ideas had at the time he came on the scene. He came on the scene when Rivers, who was then extremely influential, along with Grafton Elliott Smith and Perry, had embraced this wild functionalism, and I think

Radcliffe-Brown on the one hand, and Malinowski on the other, were a welcome corrective.

JG: Hmmm...
MNS: You want me to go on?

JG: Yes. Well, Ghurye, he wasn't influenced at all by Rivers' other interests. Because you know, Rivers of course was not only interested in diffusionism. His book on social organization was a very interesting analytical volume which, you know, in a sense, influenced, Radcliffe-Brown himself there...
MNS: On that, there are two points I'd like to make. One is that it is Ghurye who made me read his copy of kinship and social organization.

JG: It was...yes...yes...
MNS: There were a few lectures meant to be given at Calcutta or somewhere. Anyway, I read them. Ghurye himself was deeply interested in the field of kinship, an interest which he pursued for a long time. And he has written a paper on dual organization in India. This interest was there. What is the other book? Social organization?

JG: Yes.
MNS: Social organization. He was a bit less enthusiastic, let me put it that way. Radcliffe-Brown on the other hand was quite enthusiastic about social organization. He told me that he could point to passages in social organization which Rivers had rewritten to answer criticisms by Radcliffe-Brown.

JG: You mean, Rivers had given the manuscript to Radcliffe-Brown to read…?
MNS: Yeah. Radcliffe-Brown was convinced that had Rivers lived longer, he would have seen the light, and been converted to Radcliffe-Brownian, Durkheimian functionalism.[26]

JG: Hmmm
MNS: It's a very interesting thing. And social organization, I think, Rivers comes closest to being a sociologist, I would say. It was obvious that, to me, that Radcliffe-Brown had been in touch with Rivers. As to the extent of the influence Radcliffe-Brown wielded on Rivers in his last phase, this is a matter for research.

Stephen Levinson (SL): Did Ghurye dominate Indian anthropology at that time?

MNS: Well, actually Ghurye, I would say, was probably the single most important influence in Indian sociology and anthropology. And one of the good things in India is, you can be a sociologist and do anthropological work, and you can be a social anthropologist and do sociological work. This is, one of the main factors in it, is the influence of Ghurye, because Ghurye, he could write on the disposal of the human placenta in India, you know, that was one of his interests and then Indo-European kinship on the other. And he could also write about cities, about *sadhus*, about caste and race in India. So, he was a kind of.... What is the word for it...? Polymath...?

SL: Yeah.

MNS: And his basic training had been in Sanskrit. He got his Master's in Sanskrit. Bombay then had a very good tradition in Sanskrit learning and teaching, and I think Ghurye got the Chancellor's Medal. Then he came under the influence of Patrick Geddes, who was appointed in 1914, as the Director of the School of Economics and Sociology in Bombay. For some odd reason, he was brought in and given charge of a research institution, without emphasis on day-to-day teaching. This was one of the best things that happened in the social sciences in India.

Ghurye, after a year with Geddes,[27] he went to Hobhouse[28] in London and found Hobhouse monumentally dull. So, he left him after I think six months or a year. And then, came to Cambridge where he came under the influence of Rivers and Haddon. There he was completely overwhelmed by Rivers' personality, and he told me that, after meeting Rivers, he was walking along, maybe Trinity Street, and he saw a copy of Rivers' latest publication, *Instinct and the Unconscious*.[29] He read it, and he told Rivers he had read it, and he asked Ghurye what he thought of it. Ghurye said, 'It's very good, but it is mechanistic', which I thought was very, you know, you need a lot of....what's the word....spunk to tell a man like Rivers that your book is mechanistic, you know, when you've just come from India and so on.

Apparently, this made Rivers like Ghurye, and he allowed Ghurye to submit a couple of papers, long papers for his PhD. Ghurye told me that one of the disasters in his life was to see St John's flag flying half-mast one morning. Rivers had died suddenly on the operation theatre, operating table of strangulated hernia. And Ghurye felt orphaned as he told me, but apparently, Rivers had spoken to Haddon about Ghurye, and Ghurye finished his thesis and got back to Bombay to the, as it then was, the School of Economics and Sociology.

And subsequently, though he himself was a non-chair sociologist, he built up a sociological tradition based on fieldwork. He knew that India had started to change in a big way. He would get his students, on the one hand, to dig up data from tribes and castes, reports, gazetteers, travellers' accounts etcetera, etcetera. And on the other, to do fieldwork. But I think I was probably one of the students whom he wanted to go in for intensive fieldwork. I remember receiving a letter from him in the field when I told him that I had gathered, I think, I was given to bragging, I said, I had gathered a tremendous amount of data. He wrote back promptly saying, remember Malinowski. It was a gentle, but a very firm snub and you know, it taught me the virtues of modesty, I think.

Anyway, I think I have done with Ghurye. And Ghurye said that Radcliffe-Brown was the person I should go to. I think he found Malinowski.... He didn't like Malinowski partly because Malinowski was so critical of Rivers, whereas Radcliffe-Brown had been....

This kind of bond is recognized in Indian learning. If you are the student of the same teacher, you are called *guru-bhai*, that is, brothers of the same *guru*. He recommended me to his *guru-bhai*. Radcliffe-Brown left Oxford in '46 July. He recommended me to Evans-Pritchard. He told Evans-Pritchard that he should take me on, and it was under Evans-Pritchard, that I finished my thesis on the Coorgs.

And Evans-Pritchard threw a lot of cold water on Durkheim, and Evans-Pritchard thought that I was too enthusiastic in my embrace of functionalism, and he wanted to gently introduce some scepticism into my frame of mind which I think he did succeed, over a longer period of time. But I found that Evans-Pritchard... Evans-Pritchard pooh-poohed Durkheim, but if you read his Nuer religion and see his chapter on Nuer sacrifice, it takes a tremendous amount from Durkheim. I think Evans-Pritchard, at that phase in his life, was rejecting Durkheim because of his determinism, but it did not mean that he rejected the sounder portions in Durkheim's sociology.

Anyway, to cut a long story short, I got my degree in July '47, and Evans-Pritchard was present when I was conferred the degree, because I was his first PhD baby in Oxford. I have, you know, I was, in a sense, the last student of Radcliffe-Brown in Oxford, and the first of Evans-Pritchard. And it was Evans-Pritchard who created the job for me in Oxford, as university lecturer in Indian sociology. One of the attractions of the job was, I got this letter when I was in India, he gave the first year of my job, he told me, that I could spend a year doing fieldwork in an Indian village, because I had told him that I felt very keenly the lack of really intensive fieldwork. And he said, 'Why don't you do it while you are there, instead of coming here and then going back after a year'.

I was delighted with this offer. It illustrates how thoughtful Evans-Pritchard could be when it came to helping a younger colleague student.

I regard my ten and a half months in Rampura[30] as probably one of the most important periods in my life. I did do fairly serious intensive fieldwork. My whole knowledge of India, in a sense, underwent a change as a result of this experience. It is because of that, that I'm an ardent advocate of experience of intensive fieldwork, whether one is doing social anthropology or sociology in India.

This is particularly necessary for Indians because, by and large, the kind of students who come into higher learning in India, whether it's social anthropology or physics, come from the urban middle classes and upper class, and they have very little knowledge of India. In fact, very little knowledge, except in the case of some students coming from traditional groups, very little knowledge of their traditional culture, and still less of rural areas. And finally, living in a caste cum class society, you unconsciously imbibe a certain negative attitude towards the culture of lower groups. And the one way of getting all this negative stuff out of them, is to send them to a village or tribe or urban slum.

I don't know if any of you have seen my book, which I edited along with two of my colleagues two years ago, *The Fieldworker and the Field.*[31] It consists of 18 statements of intensive field experiences in different settings, 16 of them are based on Indian experience, and they include not only working in village India and tribal India, but also urban slums, factories, trade unions, small-town politics, *nari samaj*[32] neighbourhood unit, the range and diversity of the experience, going into a matrilineal area in a very traditional part of Palghat[33] in southern Kerala. The range of experience is astonishing. I would make it compulsory reading for anybody taking up social anthropology or sociology, not because I'm one of its editors, but I do think that Indian students, particularly, need to be brought out of their domestic and caste and sectarian shells, to appreciate this richness and diversity of Indian culture. And also, much more important, to see that multiplicity of perceptions is basic to Indian society and culture. I don't know if I'm making sense to you....

JG: How have you managed in India? You say it was partly due to Ghurye that you have in a sense this overlapping fields of sociology and social anthropology, and I think, it's significant that you said yourself, that, you know, you found Radcliffe-Brown an interesting, or interesting from the standpoint of here, you came across a true sociology. It is significant too, I think, that your lectureship in Oxford was a lectureship in Indian sociology.

Now although we have got this tradition, I think Radcliffe-Brown himself spoke of comparative sociology, and when anyone asked me what I am, I speak in the same kind of terms. On the other hand, it's a very difficult situation to maintain, because the sort of 'polarization' takes place. Anthropologists inevitably get stigmatized as they do in current disputes in this country, as blue lagoon anthropologists. And students themselves see two channels. One which involves going to far-off places and blue lagoons, and the other which involves working in your slum areas. We get too little of the latter nowadays.

JG: How do you manage to keep some kind of balance, overlap? How have you managed to achieve this greater overlap in India because in many other countries, there has been this greater polarity really, that's taken place with sociology being defined as, you know, the here now, the active part of things, with social anthropology being involved in rural areas' more historic problems and so on, so forth...

MNS: Not that the second variety of sociology is not present in India. I mean you do get, especially students who have been to American universities and got their PhD there, they use survey research techniques and they use sampling and statistical methods and techniques much more than the anthropologists. And they are also able to produce books and papers more, I won't say easily, there is more of it in India than from social anthropologists proper. This kind of sociology is often put in opposition to social anthropology by the practitioners of sociology. I've had the distinction of being disowned both by sociologists and social anthropologists in India.

JG: That's a very honourable position....

MNS: There are certain tendencies, or rather features in Indian culture itself which enable you to, which force you to come out of your preoccupation with tribes or with urban people, to go back into history. For instance, Ghurye's own influence is very significant in this connection, and the fact that traditional life is so prominent in Indian life. And if you are investigating any section of Indian life, you come into contact with the book dimension, as I call it, with the scriptural dimension, and you come into contact with rituals specially, and you go to pilgrim centres where they have your genealogical records. So, the past is ever present in India, if I may say so. You can't make a hard and fast distinction, and this is one of the factors which makes it very difficult to divide the field neatly between anthropologists and sociologists.

And not only Ghurye but some of the other sociologists like Chattopadhyay who was also a student of Rivers in Calcutta, and N.K. Bose.[34] N.K. Bose, for instance, studied tribals, and he also studied coronation rituals in Orissa. He didn't publish much though, but this to-ing and fro-ing between tribes and aspects of traditional culture, studying pilgrimage centres and so on. The presence of tradition in a very strong and in a very live manner in Indian culture is certainly a factor, I think.

And apart from it, I have, you know, another idea which I find very useful. Another idea of Radcliffe-Brown, is this concept of comparative sociology. The only thing is it's not practiced anywhere but it's useful as in polemics when you're fighting for the right kind of sociology or anthropology, to call yourself a comparative sociologist, which ideally includes all societies in space and time. And that is to say, you can work for instance in ancient India, I mean, you can discuss the role of Buddhism in ancient Indian society, or Jainism in ancient Indian society. Arvind Shah, for instance, who has done probably one of the best village studies in India, did a study on a multi-caste village in Kheda district.[35] He is deeply interested in history. He has written several papers in what I call sociological history and he is bringing out a collection of his papers on sociological history, with the special area being Gujarat.

I would argue for comparative sociology, and this also enables me to have a dialogue with historians, with demographers, with economic historians, and others. Sociology, as it is developing in India, has a continuing dialogue with these people. It's not enough, I think, we should have more of that dialogue. And on the other hand, you have linkages with, within quotes, Indologists, Sanskritists and specialists on Buddhism, Jainism and so on. As I see it, you have to work with the social sciences, and you have to work with the Indologists, and you also are interested in tribes. Many of these tribes have some Hindu traits in them. You remember one of the criticisms of Mauss[36] I don't know how justified it is, of Rivers' work on the Todas, is that Rivers ignores the influence of Hinduism on the Todas.

When these tribes live cheek by jowl with Hindus, they do, there's a continuous interaction between the two. There is not only Hinduization of tribal groups, but at the lower levels of Hindu society itself, tribal elements are quite strong. We can't ignore this element. Apart from it, historically speaking, many of the dominant castes of India have come from the ranks of tribes, so given such a culture's civilization, I think any kind of sharp differentiation between sociologists who study sectors of urban society and anthropologists who studied tribes would be artificial and I think....

JG: Well, I think that's true, but on the other hand, it has been possible elsewhere, and it's interesting that hasn't happened in India. Whereas I can remember a few years ago, when André Béteille[37] was visiting here, doing his best to persuade Dr Humphrey and I to get people to go to the sort of central areas of Hinduism rather than going up to the tribes, because we think we found that colleagues who worked in Nepal, not here, really wanted to go to some peripheral area of India or else they wanted to get into tribal areas and after all Radcliffe-Brown himself worked on the Andaman Islanders which was hardly a central area in our Indian experience. There was, you know, there was a lot of push, I think, still, for that... and it's very interesting I think that Indian anthropology...

SL: I think, one of the distinctive things of Indian anthropology is so many members of the profession work on their own culture. I mean, that breaks down the barrier.

JG: What was your relationship with Coorg and Rampura?

MNS: My relationship with Coorg, unfortunately, I visited it incognito a few years ago, but I really want to go there, once announcing that... Coorgs know about me...

JG: I really meant... I was taking after Stephen's point there... you weren't going back to your own culture in Coorg?

MNS: No... no... no...

JG: I'm sorry I was....

SL: Yes, so, how in a sense I suppose, there seem to be a lot of difficulties about working in your own culture. At least that's part of the set of beliefs I think that we labour under, namely that one doesn't have perhaps the perspective that one would be working as an outsider. Secondly, perhaps there'd be actual difficulties working as a participant observer in a circumstance in which one is already a part of the system. Did these difficulties beset you or is it because Indian society is so fragmented, one is always an outsider...?

MNS: Let me put it this way. There are difficulties for the insider, and a certain amount of discipline, rather, let me put it differently: an anthropologist should have experience of a different culture before he gets to his own. But then India is, you said, fragmented, I would look at it differently, so rich in diversity. When you send somebody in Bombay to a tribe in Kerala you are not sending him to his own culture.

This tribe is really very backward and its lifestyle is so completely different from that of a Bombay youth or Calcutta youth. You needn't even go that far. You take a student in Bangalore and take him ten miles away. If he's a Kannada speaker, you can take him to the Telugu area, if he is a Tamil speaker you can take him into the Kannada area, because Bangalore is a tri-junction of Kannada, Telugu and Tamil.

In fact, you can do a lot of backyard anthropology in India. It is so rich in diversity that you are at once a stranger and the surprises you get, you know, if one is sufficiently reflective, and I hope anthropology students are sufficiently reflective, that is, you tell yourself after a while, 'Why I thought I knew this culture, but I don't know anything about it'.

Let me tell you a thing that happened to me: this was not my first fieldwork, this was really my second fieldwork, after I had done my Coorg fieldwork. Rampura is only 22 miles from Mysore, and during the summer of 1948, there was a protracted drought, and in this part of Mysore, you do get odd rains, a couple of rains. You are supposed to get them in the middle of April, I mean. There were no rains, and then, the summer soils were affected by it, and every day, this was the main topic of our conversation, you know, when is it going to rain, and then they even... they just used to ask everybody for signs of rain and so on... I won't go into it. But after a while, I mean when it was close to May I think, they decided to go and consult one of the deities in the village, about the prospects for rain, and the deity in question is in the form of a stone bull.

This stone bull represents Nandi which is the vehicle of Shiva, and Nandi in this part of India, is associated with the cattle, with agriculture, with fodder, the whole lot. It's a very, very relevant deity to the peasants of this region. I was told about it, and I accompanied the party of village elders who went to consult the deity. I thought they would have some prayer, respectfully, and then ask. I didn't know how the deity would give an answer, and they told me that the deity would answer their query. We went there, it was a very warm day, very hot, and it's a stone temple and we got in there, with no windows. And then there was this deity with, you know, flowers had been arranged, and there was a priest, very elderly Lingayat priest. He waved the camphor around it thrice, and then the audience sat, and they were to make the request. The leader of the delegation, a man in his 70s then, he said in a very matter of fact way, 'Come on, give us an answer!' addressing the stone image. I was taken aback, I was wondering you see, how the answer would be given.

Somebody explained to me that if one of the arranged flowers on the right side fell, it meant a *yes*, and if another flower on the left side fell, it meant *no*. And one of them told me, on occasion, you'll even see a flower being flung at you. I was waiting for the flower to be flung at me, and nothing happened. And the peasants became very angry. And then this elder barked at the deity, 'Who do you think we are, we are not ordinary people, we are important people, we have come to ask you a question. If you are going to say no, well, give us a clear no. Don't keep us waiting!'

And then, the next question was, you know, I'm paraphrasing, what I have written. The next question was even more interesting: 'Are you a deity or are you a stone image?' At this question, my initial impulse was to burst out laughing, but then, I sensed the mood of the villagers. They were in deadly earnest, you see. They had no doubt that they were conversing with a God, and no reply was given. And then somebody said they would come the following morning for a cold shower, but they didn't, and we dispersed. But take this brief experience of mine. I don't think if you are brought up in an urban area, you'd have any notion of it.

Or my other experience in Coorg when I found this oracle who had been fasting for days, and the people knew his movements you know. As though they had a script giving them his movements. They said he'll come and he will put out this fire and they saw a man in a white gown and open Coorg sword in his hand, and then, I remember the fire, which was of timber logs, and I couldn't stand. As the fire got going, I started, you know, moving away from it, and I measured it. At about ten feet, it was too hot for me to stand near it, so I moved away.

This man came and with bare feet, he jumped on it, and with bare feet, he almost stamped out the fire. And then he went to the front of the temple, stood on the verandah and then started gashing himself with the sword, and then, I saw blood streaming. It's a very unnerving sight. And then, in emulation of him, the untouchable oracles below started gashing themselves, and then, at the next moment, he was inside the main temple, and outside the sanctum sanctorum and there he was gashing himself. At one point, the young Brahmin priest of the temple came, and then he said, 'This man is supposed to be possessed by Bhadrakali', and this boy spoke in Kodagu. He said, 'We have had your visit, we hope you are not angry, you calm down now, and leave us in peace…'. They gave the consecrated water, and the oracle took it and then it subsides, you know, he resumed his normal self.

I mean I think this would be an absolutely strange experience for most Indians. So, the point I'm making is, India is so diverse and varied, regionally and sectorally or caste-wise and ethnic group-wise that I don't think this argument about insider and outsider is….

SL: What about caste affiliations? Caste affiliations... those of us who could even come from the outside find that once we start getting associated with a particular caste, we find we have limited access to other castes. Now already coming in with a caste… already coming in with a caste assignation of some sort… did you find that?

MNS: Actually, what happened was that the villagers in Rampura made me behave like a Brahmin. They found me a very... I would call myself a relaxed Brahmin. They thought I was not really the thing, and the headman's daughter, the headman from the dominant Vokkaliga[38] caste. His daughter was 10, was shocked about my indifference to pollution and purity. And she would go home and regale them with tales of my, you know, ignorance of these rules. And then of course they were, you know, I couldn't have been a non-vegetarian in the village. And when guests came from the city the headman, even as the jeep was coming in, the headman would have known the castes of, I mean I'm exaggerating a bit, the occupants or the passengers and tell me that I would be feeding the Brahmins, and he would take care of the others. It was there, and if I had rejected this role, my access to everybody would have been shut.

But on the other hand, I wanted to visit the Harijan[39] area, and I asked the headman because I knew I needed his permission to do anything. And if I had not asked him, if I incurred his wrath, he could have me thrown out of the village within 24 hours. He kept postponing it, so one day after a while, I walked with my assistant to the Harijan area, and started, you know, in the verandah of every hut, and asked them about their genealogies, you know, their land and other data, their occupations etc., which really was a very lucky thing I did, because it made the untouchables feel that I was not a creature of the headman's, that I was free. So, I think you have to play it by ear. You cannot afford to displease the dominant caste, but also, at some point, this is a matter for individual judgment, you should make everybody know that you are there to learn from everybody, and then, here there are certain idioms one has to use. The headman asked me one day, I mean the headman was barely literate, he asked me, 'Why are you collecting all this data?' You know, he thought of me, you know, I could have been employed more usefully.... 'Why are you doing this?'

I said, 'Look, there are so many changes occurring in the lives of the villagers, that I feel that you know that I should record them. Your grandchildren will probably find the village much changed'. At once, he replied, 'Oh you are doing something like the early Chinese travellers who have left records of India in the ancient days'.

I was amazed at his perceptiveness, that you are a learner. Incidentally it is in line with the Brahminical role you see, to be a learner. At a certain stage, I got very interested in the settlement of disputes. I went and told my young friends there, 'I want to be present at some disputes. I don't come to know about their occurrence. Will you teach me?' They took me in hand. Their way of making me learn was they would take me straight into a dispute, a street dispute, and say these are the facts, as the dispute was going on. 'Give, you know, give your verdict.' I would venture forth with some answer, and they would shoot it down, and start laughing. This is with all your degrees and so on, you are giving such a foolish judgment.

You know, they hide relevant facts from me. But after a while, I realized it as a game that was being played in which they wanted to make me out to be a fool, but as long as I was willing to go along with them in this game, I learned more and more about, you know, dispute settlement, and I found it very useful to play the role of the fool. And in essence I was. I knew very little about the village.

Member of audience: How important did you find it personally in doing your fieldwork, to have close relations with one or two individuals who..., or perhaps more than that, who would really give you a sort of psychological idea of what was happening there, as opposed to an undifferentiated relationship with lot of different people? Because I remember, you wrote about this in your book, *The Remembered Village,* you described, there were one or two people who were particularly important to you...three...yes...

MNS: In essence, with the second man, my assistant, the man who appointed himself my assistant, I had no choice at all, and he just came and appointed himself, and he proved to be extremely useful.

JG: Radin... Paul Radin.[40]

MNS: Radin belonged to the intellectual class. He was curious about customs, and so on, and he was also, what the Americans would call, an oddball. He didn't fit into village society. He had a low reputation. At the time I met him I didn't know that you know. He'd squandered away his inheritance and was living on his wits. He was extremely useful to me. He would give me a comment on what was going on, behind the scenes. But then, after a while I realized that he had his interest too. The thing is, every man projects a view which is somehow related to, not only his perceptions, he has interests, and my friend Kulle Gowda, I would say, that he, on occasion, promoted a dispute because he would get an opportunity to write documents and make some money, and have influence with people and so on. This was one of the sources.

But the other one, Nadu Gowda, the elder among the Vokkaliga, he was extremely knowledgeable about village life. And he was also a great friend of mine. With all the three people, I was not only a learner, I had some kind of emotional bond with them. I also had friendships in the village, and as you probably know by now, that you do not have any privacy in an Indian village, especially if you are a bachelor, as I then was. They were with me from morning till night, and all my notes had to be written while somebody was looking over my shoulder, and it was only at night, I used to bolt my door and write under the light of two hurricane lanterns. Sometimes the headman would have borrowed one, I had to write under the light of one lantern.

One night, I remember, I was very tired, and I was sleeping, or trying to sleep, when I got a knock on the door and he kept on asking for me, 'Swami... Swami' and so on. It's a respectful term for addressing a Brahmin, incidentally. I didn't answer because I wanted to sleep. And then, he went around to the window on the side and peered through it, and started shouting louder. After a while, I couldn't resist him. I opened the door. I thought there was some emergency and you know, maybe somebody was sick. I used to have a lot of tablets and medicines for that, and I asked him, 'Ira Gowda what do you want?' He said that he was bored, 'I thought I would have some company'.

It's 10 o' clock, past 10. By 8:00–8:30, the villagers are asleep. And then we started talking and then, we got on to discussing a famous wrestling match in Mysore in the '20s. I'd heard about it as a boy you see, a child, and I remembered everything. Wasn't the name of the wrestler so and so…? And then this man proceeded to show the trick, wrestling trick, which the local hero had used to defeat the champion from outside, from Hyderabad or somewhere. And then, around 11 o' clock or so, he was holding me like this (hands above his head). Happy villager. Then after this social visit was over, I slept very soundly.

So, what I mean is, I have identified a disease, social claustrophobia, which hits everybody in an Indian village, when we are doing fieldwork. I used to sneak away on lonely walks, and if it became unbearable, I'd go to Mysore for a day or so. I think you live very much at their mercy. I've heard of Africans telling me that they would close their doors at 10 o'clock and type till late into the night. I don't think one could do it in an Indian village.

JG: I don't know who these Africans were. They were very lucky to have doors, in my experience.

Member of audience: Professor Srinivas, you mentioned you made many friends in the village and you had certain people with whom you exchanged a lot of information, but did you find that, by making friendships with certain people, you alienated other people and what did you do about that?

MNS: This is a very good question, if I may say so, because I've heard social scientists, anthropologists saying that I kept so many families under observation. In my case, the opposite was true. The headman had kept me under observation within a couple of hours of my leaving....

JG: Three hundred families were keeping you under observation...

MNS: I'd been told that this village had no factions and so on. Actually, I thought for a while, whether I should go to such an atypical village. If there were no factions, you know, it would not be worth studying. But very soon, within a few hours of my arrival, I knew there were factions. One of the young faction leaders, he called himself a member of the Indian National Congress Party. He was one of the Young Turks. He told me, 'You are staying near the headman and doubtless, he will tell you about what's going on in the village. It will be a very one-sided view of the village. If you are going to write a dispassionate account about our village, how do you make sure you will listen to everybody?' I told him, 'I would like to talk to you very much. This is exactly what I come to this village for. When are you free, I would like an appointment with you?' I think this disarmed him a bit and he became a kind of friend of mine.

But subtler than this was the fact that Nadu Gowda's sons were opposed to the headman and his rule, and they were leaders in a faction opposed to the headman. They were some of my best informants and friends. I used to go to them and I used to relax with them. The headman and his family were always, you know, reserved whereas, with this group, they were not so reserved, and I used to drink tea with them, go for long walks with them and so on. The headman was always suspicious of my association with them and he would ask me, question me, on what we talked about and so on. I would tell him, not the strict truth, but something like, we were talking about ritual and this and that.

But, once I really fell afoul of the headman, and it was due entirely to my thoughtlessness. This was years after I'd left the village. I was on a brief visit, and I think the normal caution which I exercised, had left me, and one group of brothers were bitterly opposed to the headman. They said, the moment they saw me get off the bus, they said, will you come and photograph a part of the embankment of the village tank. It's very important to us. I thought it was an innocent question. I went and took photographs and they told me that the tank water had gushed through a hole and ruined their crop and so on. They asked me to send photographs of the breach in the embankment etc. etc., which I promised to do.

Then I went to pay my respects to the headman. The headman said, 'What have you been doing?' He was very curt with me, 'What have I been doing?' I said, 'I went to the tank and I've photographed the embankment and...'.

He said, 'Do you know they are having a case against us? They've sued the panchayat for nuisance or something, and they are going to use you and your photographs as evidence against us. Do you think it's loyal on your part to do this to us, you see?' It was comeuppance of the kind I'd never thought would happen. I, at once, apologized to him, and I told him that I would tear up the negatives, which I did.

So, you have to be very, very careful, in walking the edge of factionalism, as it were. It's a very real danger. But on the other hand, the headman didn't mind, or couldn't prevent me from being very friendly with the untouchables. There was one young rebel among the untouchables, who was very witty, and very articulate and he used to give it to the landowners, or rather his landowner. In a particular dispute I witnessed, I mean, he scored so many points, that many landowners started admiring his wit, his logic, and so on.

This is another feature of Indian village life that there is a certain aesthetic appreciation of disputes and arguments. And the man who argues cleverly is admired and so on. He didn't mind my going to different castes, but he certainly minded me going to the opposite faction.

Member of Audience: We've received warnings about problems for Western anthropologists moving upwards or downwards, is really not the thing. It's a question of moving sideways where the real problem lies which is...

MNS: I would say, both ways. This is why one has to be continually on the watch about how one behaves. One is supposed to be relaxing, but even when one is relaxing with friends, one should be careful about what one says. At any moment you might hurt somebody. There's no book which can help. I think it's some kind of increased sensitivity. I think this is why I found this, and the amount of data I had to collect and record. About once in, between four to six weeks, I would have difficulties in sleeping. I would then go back to Mysore, probably sleep for a day or so, and then come back refreshed. I don't know Jack, what's your experience? I think one has to be on the alert all the time. And it's part of the strain of fieldwork.

JG: Yes, it's true, though I prefer it myself to other sorts of strain. I regard it as a pleasure....

MNS: Oh yeah!

Alan Macfarlane: Another aspect of being on your guard... These are again to do with the ethics of fieldwork. There are two problems which I wondered whether you could comment on... one is, in the past, in a lot of the anthropology that was written by colonialists, who went out to a place, they came back and they wrote about the natives never expecting either to see the natives again, or certainly not expecting the natives to read their books. I wondered your situation, where you were very close in many ways to the people, and they were quite likely to be affected by what you wrote and to read possibly, what you wrote, you mentioned this Coorg return, whether that affects much more how you report, because so much more has to be carefully weighed in terms of what effect it might have on the people. And the second question is, that, and this is what is often seen as the central ethical question in anthropology, the manipulation of people as a source of data. In other words, I find even now, 10 years after having done fieldwork in Nepal, when people from the field write to me, I get a peculiar sense of guilt, almost.... These are people who provided me with material for my own work. Often, they write with requests, which I'm unable to fulfil or don't feel like I can fulfil well enough. But I'm a long way away, I'm thousands of miles away. I wondered whether the problem of both having people as friends, and people who you enter into human relationships with, and also as people who are ultimately objects of study, which is greater for you?

MNS: In a sense, it imposed a terrible strain on me, because to regard Nadu Gowda, Kulle Gowda or the headman as only sources of data was aberrant to me, because they were human beings and I had close and intimate links with them, as with my friends. But my role was that of the learner, and I could ask them questions, and they liked teaching me, that's also another thing. But there is a seamy side to data. It was when asking about that that I've been most uncomfortable.

JG: Seamy side?

MNS: Seamy side... yes, for instance, a dispute would have taken place. Who is sleeping with who you see, or did that man say that, make that statement because he had been spurned by that wife or widow... This, I found very unpleasant to ask. I would ask occasionally Kulle Gowda. Even he showed a reluctance to answer it, because, in asking this question, I had somehow come down in his eyes as it were. He had this image of me as a scholar, as a decent human being, and to ask this question was a strain on me, and for him to answer. But sometimes he answered, and sometimes he didn't.

There is one problem particularly when you are discussing inter-caste relations, and as anyone who knows an Indian village, you hear stories about so and so being the keep of so and so, and so on. You know these stories are abundant, and either you say that such rumours are widespread, or if you want to find out if it is really true, how do you do it. I found asking these questions very unpleasant, and the only occasion I could ask such questions was from one of my friends, when I was out on a walk with him, and then after we had talked about other things, to slowly turn the conversation around to this. The collection of information was unpleasant for me. To this extent, I may have failed as a fieldworker. That is one.

And second, I did find that my being friends with them minimized the manipulative element in my fieldwork. I would run errands for them, I'd give them gifts whenever I went to Mysore. I knew one of the things the village lacked was fresh vegetables and fruits. I would take fresh vegetables and fruits, and distribute it among my friends. Continually, I would have this problem of how do I repay them, am I doing the right thing, and I did try to help, but ultimately the question is that there is the question of manipulation. I mean, there is a fact of manipulation by the anthropologists of the indigenes. It's a very unpleasant affair, and it is unpleasant for me particularly, because I feel I am very close to them. I have some ideas for atoning for my sins, but that will have to be done in the future.

JG: Markus, were you going to ask about the ethics of fieldwork or...?

Markus Banks: I was thinking more about the distancing effect as it were. You were talking earlier with Stephen, about sending out students into their own backyards as it were, but you still make it apparent that they've got to go to a different culture area or language area. And you were saying that you yourself went back to Mysore to sort of recuperate and sleep. Does anybody in India actually work literally with their own culture? Do you think that's possible or even desirable?

MNS: I think it is necessary at some point to look at your own culture. Because anthropology can't always be of the other culture. But to do your own culture calls for certain habits of mind and thought. This distancing, of looking at your culture, as an outsider I think, has to be done. In a talk I gave which published selectively, it's distributed among a few people, there I discussed the development of the fieldworker in the field.

The first stage was bewilderment, 'once bornness', I called it. The second stage, this great rapport which you think you have, I called 'twice bornness', so much so, that you look at the world from the point of view of the indigenes, and you think everything they do is right, and everything the outsider, the official, the visitor, or even you, do is wrong. But I think 'twice bornness' is not enough. It may be enough for a Brahmin, it's not enough for an anthropologist. He has to be thrice born, and he has to go back and distance himself from the field. And one process, I mean, two necessary acts in distancing: one is to run away from the field, physical distancing is absolutely necessary. You must get away from that environment. And two, writing is distancing. The discipline of writing, and writing for an audience of anthropologists, each of whom has his own group and has done or is about to do the distancing. These two are necessary. And after you've done probably one or two people, then you can take on your own culture. Not before that.

Member of Audience: Peter Berger,[41] for instance, has his idea of disillusioning – that as a sociologist you finally come to see your own society from outside. But he doesn't feel it's necessary to go off to New Guinea or somewhere before you can do that. You would regard it as essential to leave your own culture before...?

MNS: Not to go to New Guinea. For instance, let me say, let me take up an area that I know nothing about, and say a middle-class student here could study a slum, if you wanted to go to New Guinea, you could go to Leicester and study the Gujaratis – that would be a different enough culture. So, then he could go back and study his own people.

Markus Banks: In fact, I am going off to Leicester....

MNS: You are going off to Leicester, you're doing the right thing.

JG: I'm glad you see it that way!

Member of Audience: Professor Srinivas, do you find that...if you're seeking explanation from your villagers you get different explanations from different people, and does that mean that you had to, kind of, work out the psychology of each informer, before you can evaluate what exactly are they saying?

MNS: Not only psychology, you know, you have to know his interests, his occupation, land rights, his relations with his kinsfolk, his friends, which statement comes from a particular personality and a whole matrix of context. So, the explanation itself needs a comment, and an explanation. Am I making sense or...?

Member of Audience: Yes, but like you mentioned about the fact that the village headman said that there were no factions. Are there events which, after a period, they begin to deny that these happened, and gloss over things, so that it's presented in a very different way by the same people over time.

MNS: I think there are two or three things here. One, any outsider, when they are faced with any outsider, especially with an outsider whom they respect, the standard rhetoric is we are no factions. Because anything which does not create a positive image in your mind about the village, they would not tell you. In fact, within two days of my coming, I knew that somebody had set fire to somebody's hay rick, and the matter was mentioned in my presence. But when I tried to ask for details about it, I was just, you know, they just turned to some other topic. It was weeks later that I started to know about who had set fire to whose hay rick, and so on. The point is, gradually as you are absorbed into the village, then you are told more and more things. But even then, in the last analysis, they remember that you are an outsider, and they won't tell everything to you. Because of my many contacts and my friends amongst the younger villagers, and I think, in a sense, they meant it, I think, there was a compliment implied in this, they said, as I was leaving the village, 'You know so much about our village you can get every one of us into trouble you see'. So, there is that fear.

Also, on the one hand, they want to present a decent image of their village to you. On the other hand, if you know too much, then you can get them into trouble. For instance, there was not a single landowner who had not encroached on government land, you see. And I had land figures. I knew the survey numbers of each villager. I could say you know where exactly they could have encroached upon. But they didn't know one thing, even if I made a report about it, the government officials would know that this was universal, and it was silly on their part to try and prevent this. They would have that much sense, I gather.

JG: I wonder if I could take you away from the problems of fieldwork, because get a group of anthropologists together, and they always want to ask.... Really, they are asking about their own experience rather than yours. I wonder if I could ask you what it was that led you into doing sociology in the first place, when you said you went to work with Ghurye in Bombay?

MNS: You know, at a purely secular rational level, I would say, accident. By this I mean I was lucky enough to have malaria around the time I passed the matriculation exam, and I was thought to be very delicate by my family. They said, 'This boy is not tough enough to do Medicine, so let him go to the Arts'. That was one, and second, after I passed my intermediate examination, and, I didn't do very well in it for various reasons. My brother asked a friend of his, 'Now look what should Chamu do for the BA'. That friend was a Marxist, and he used to recite revolutionary Marxist songs on Sacco and Vanzetti.[42] They were...

JG: I recall yeah...

MNS: ...and he was a friend of my brother's. My brother had friends in all places, and he asked me to produce the handbook of the University of Mysore. I went through the BA Honours courses. There was social philosophy and it was an encyclopaedic course, designed by Anil Seal's[43] grandfather I suspect, or he had a hand in it. It included, apart from English and the second language Kannada or Sanskrit, it included the minor subjects: social psychology, social anthropology, comparative political institutions and economics or something. Then as major subjects, philosophy of religion, political philosophy, ethics, history of ethics, Indian social institutions, Indian ethics and essays.... So, Acharya, that was my brother's friend, said, 'This is a very humanizing course, why don't you go through it?' And my brother said, 'Why don't you take it?'

You see, you know, remembering that I was too delicate to do Medicine, so I went on to social philosophy. There I got really some kind of background, I won't say grounding, and it was there that I heard about Ghurye and his eminence. And it was in my first or second-year BA Honours course that the names of Rivers,

Malinowski and so on became familiar to me. Then I went to Ghurye. Ghurye was our examiner at the final year Honours, and he had given me first-class marks. Normally you are not allowed to do a Master's degree in sociology in Bombay without taking eight papers over a period of two years.

He said, 'You have done, you've covered the ground, so why don't you do it by dissertation?' This was due to the fact that Ghurye didn't want me to waste my time, and also because he sensed that I had read too much theory and highfalutin things, and that I should be rooted to or rooted in facts. And you know, what he did? The first book he gave me to read was Hobhouse's *Morals in Evolution*, which very nearly put me off sociology. Have you seen that book?

JG: Yes... I have.
MNS: Don't tell me you prescribed it?

JG: I find other ways of boring the students.

SL: Going back to those early times... You were doing your graduate work during a momentous period of Indian history gaining of Independence. So, was anthropology probably associated with the British Raj in any way? Was that a factor at all?
MNS: Yeah... Anthropology was, and the members of the Indian National Congress[44] were opposed to, you know. I see sufficient stern anthropologists, and at that time they were arguing for a separate status for tribals, the need for tribals to be protected from the plains Hindus. In the 1935 Act, there were two categories: one, the Scheduled Castes, that is the untouchables, and the other, the Scheduled Areas. These areas were areas where the tribals lived. You'll be surprised to learn that about 18 miles from Bombay's Thana, where tribals lived, the Warlis[45] and others, that was excluded from the limited provincial autonomy offered under the 1935 Government of India Act. So Indian nationalists were opposed to anthropology.

SL: I see...
MNS: But you know Ghurye himself...

JG: They were opposed to setting aside these areas because they wanted it done on a regional basis...
MNS: They thought it was a ruse of the...

JG: Yes, yes.... to divide and...
MNS: To divide and to keep the tribals to themselves. Ghurye wrote a book based entirely on secondary sources, on the Scheduled Tribes and their future. It showed that the problems of the tribals in many ways were similar to those of the poorer peasants, and it didn't make sense to separate them. So that way, he won acceptance at the hands of the Indians as well. Ghurye didn't do it for a dishonest reason, I mean, Ghurye would not do anything dishonest like that. He was really convinced that there was so much of tribal culture which was in common with the culture of the so-called lower groups and vice-versa, that it was artificial to separate them. Then there was Vaikunth Mehta, not Vaikunth Mehta... Thakkar Bapa,[46] whom Elwin[47] also mentions, who had dedicated his life to working among the tribals. There was both the nationalist approach to the tribal problem and the British approach to the tribal problem. So, there was this conflict between the two, and that conflict in a sense still continues.

SL: So, when you came back to set up your first department, was it with some opposition?
MNS: By that time things had changed. My job was to sell the idea of fieldwork, and fieldwork not in the sense of hit and run trips, you see, but really intensive field work. And I think, I laid about it with a will, as they say. I made a lot of enemies, I'm not discreet, I wrote polemical pieces criticizing armchair anthropology, and generally made a nuisance of myself, but I think it paid off in the end. And now, I mean, when I'm in a group in India, I'll take up the position that sociology is a field science and I do it deliberately, because knowing the habits of the Indian middle classes, I want to stress the need for them to go out and live with all kinds of groups...

JG: I don't think it's a feature confined to the English middle classes in any way. You find them all around. They don't know anything about the productive processes or anything like... yeah... anything

like that. But tell me, would you say something about your going back. You went to Rampura in '47…
MNS: '48. 8 January.

JG: '48. Yeah… '48… '49 and you came back to Oxford…
MNS: January 14 or 15…

JG: '49?
MNS: '49.

JG: … and you stayed in Oxford then, for…
MNS: Till '51 June, when I got the chair in Baroda.

JG: yes… and…then…
MNS: I stayed in Baroda…

JG: Then you gave up the post and your successor was Louis Dumont…[48] I had to get that in.
MNS: …and then David Pocock.[49]

JG: Yes… well. And you went from Oxford to Baroda. And how long were you there before starting working with the institute?…
MNS: You see, eight years in Baroda. It's the story of my life, if I may say so. I stayed long enough in Baroda to get a few good teachers, and to get a few good students. Arvind Shah and Narayan Sheth[50] were both my students there, and both of them have chairs now. And then, the University Grants Commission[51] which was set up in '54 or '55, '53 or '54 or '55 I'm hazy, I'm not certain of the dates. They thought so highly of the department in Baroda. Suddenly, you know, things were happening in Baroda. They gave me money for new posts, scholarships for study, including at the PhD level, and then grants for library, for lodging the library, and also money for field work etc., and money for a new building.

But then in 1959 February, I was in Delhi because Dr Rao[52] invited me to the Delhi chair. And so, just when I could have settled down, and really, you know, started doing my own work, I had to move to Delhi, where again the same situation, I had to start a new department. André [Beteille] was one of my first students, first recruitments in Delhi. And in nine years, the Delhi department you know, became so well known that it was made a Centre of Advanced Study for the teaching of sociology. We then had four professors in the department, and the number of posts was increased. We got money for a new building, we got money for research etc and also money to attract students from all over India. But then in '72, I had to leave to start a new Institute in Bangalore, and I spent six years there, and then I gave it up. I felt I was becoming increasingly alienated from my studies.

And now I have a Homi Bhabha[53] senior fellowship, and I have an honorary fellowship at the Indian Institute of Management, and the facilities to do my own work. I'm slowly catching up with material. A tremendous amount of new work has been done in India, exciting work, and I hope during the next few years, I will catch up with it, and be back in business as it were. Too much of my time had been spent in teaching, and in promoting the discipline, both in the university, inside university and outside. So much so, I don't want to look at a student now.

JG: Yes... I noticed you're looking the other way, but the... the Institute you set up in Baroda, and the school in Delhi, they both combined anthropology and sociology departments?
MNS: Actually, in Delhi, there was unfortunately already an anthropology department, I couldn't do anything about it. So... but I had friendly relationship...

JG: So, you became Professor of Sociology...?
MNS: But it did not prevent me from doing what I like. For instance, in 1968 or so, the University Grants Commission requested me to start a programme for the tribal people of north-eastern hill region, that is to say, the Khasis,[54] the Garos,[55] the Pnar[56] and Arunachal... We are getting students from those regions, and you are now getting members of these tribes becoming sociologists, and occupying positions, teaching and other positions in their own areas. This is one of the best things that happened. And you know, by and large, if you join the Delhi University sociology department, you can study a tribe, a temple town, an urban slum, a factory, anything. So, and then, the tribute to the department was paid by some members of the anthropology department, who send their sons or daughters to study sociology in the Department of Sociology.

JG: So, it's partly for that reason that your students, many of them have gone into a wide range of fields... I mean you've worked on trade unions and a whole range of activities of that kind.
MNS: The one who worked on trade unions has just been appointed to a chair in industrial relations in the management institute at Hyderabad. And I take it, you know, vain that I am, I take it as a feather in my cap. But let me stress about one aspect of my work. I always have mixed feelings. That is, it is not easy to develop, not that India didn't have a tradition of work in sociology and anthropology, but I had a specific conception of sociology and social anthropology, and I had to promote this, and promoting it in a developing country. Luckily for me, the University Grants Commission came, and the Indian Council of Social Science Research (ICSSR)[57] came, and it made it easier for me to do what I could for the disciplines.

But in the process, I feel my own work and research and reading have suffered grievously. Sometimes I feel that I shouldn't regret it, sometimes I feel I should regret it. So, mixed feelings... On the other hand, I'm quite certain that had I continued in Oxford, I might have become a much better scholar. But on the other hand, I wouldn't have the satisfaction that such as they are, which are mine today, in seeing that anybody from Cambridge or Oxford or Harvard or Yale and Chicago can go to Delhi and have a thumping good discussion on any sociological or anthropological issue. I feel my work has been rewarded, but I have regrets on the personal side. I don't know if I'm making sense to you....

Member of Audience: As a student, I can say there are no regrets from the students' side. We're very glad you stayed on.

JG; Now that you've reorganized your life in this way, and started reading all these books, and so on, perhaps you'll send a few students to come and study not with us in Cambridge, but perhaps study us in Cambridge.
MNS: Both...

JG: Awesome. Guess we ought to call it a day. Thank you very much!
MNS: Thank you very much!

NOTES

1. Wikipedia. 2020. https://en.wikipedia.org/wiki/M._N._Srinivas

2. The University of Mysore is the 6th oldest university in India and the oldest in the state of Karnataka. It was established in 1916 by then Maharaja of Mysore, Krishnaraja Wodeyar IV, after two of his educational experts (C. R. Reddy and Thomas Denham) undertook a five-year study of higher education around the world. They structured the new school to encompass elements from universities that promote original research (University of Chicago), those that emphasise extending knowledge among the people (University of Wisconsin), and those that combine intellectualism with an educational system calculated to train students for political and social life (University of Oxford and Cambridge). https://en.wikipedia.org/wiki/University_of_Mysore

3. G.S. Ghurye, see Appendix.

4. W.H.R. Rivers, see Appendix.

5. The term Kodava has two related usages. Firstly, it is the name of the Kodava language and culture followed by a number of communities from Kodagu. Secondly, within the Kodava-speaking communities and region (Kodagu) it describes the dominant Kodav people. The Kodavas (Kodava, anglicized as Coorgs) are considered a patrilineal ethno-lingual tribe from the region of Kodagu (in Karnataka state of southern India) who natively speak the Kodava language. https://en.wikipedia.org/wiki/Kodava_people

6. Madikeri (also known by its former name Mercara) is a hill station town in Madikeri taluk in Kodagu district, India. It is the headquarters of the district of Kodagu. https://en.wikipedia.org/wiki/Madikeri

7. Bronisław Malinowski, see Appendix.

8. A.R. Radcliffe-Brown, see Appendix.

9. Ruth Benedict, née Ruth Fulton, (1887–1948), American anthropologist whose theories had a profound influence on cultural anthropology, especially in the area of culture and personality. https://www.britannica.com/biography/Ruth-Benedict

10. The Todas are a pastoral tribe inhabiting the higher elevations of the Nilgiri Hills of southern India. It is unlikely that the ancestral homeland of the Todas will ever be identified conclusively, though linguistic evidence suggests a South Indian origin for the group. Other evidence, albeit circumstantial, points to Toda migrations from the Malabar coast region lying to the west of the Nilgiris. https://rb.gy/dbxzku

11. The Chenchus are a Telugu speaking food-gathering tribe living in the Nallamalai forests of Andhra Pradesh in India spread over the districts of Mahaboobnagar, Kurnool, Prakasam and Guntur. They are a conservative tribal group and have not made many changes in their lifestyle or tried to adapt to modernity. They live in the enclosed space and geography, leading a life of an unbroken continuity. http://www.peoplesoftheworld.org/hosted/chenchu/

12. (in some universities) the autumn term.

13. Numa Denis Fustel de Coulanges (1830–1889) French historian, the originator of the scientific approach to the study of history in France. https://www.britannica.com/biography/Numa-Denis-Fustel-de-Coulanges

14. *The Ancient City* (*La Cité antique*) published in 1864, is the most famous book of the French historian Numa Denis Fustel de Coulanges (1830–89). Taking inspiration from René Descartes, and based on texts of ancient historians and poets, the author investigates the origins of the most archaic institutions of Greek and Roman society. https://en.wikipedia.org/wiki/La_Cité_antique

15. Émile Durkheim, see Appendix.

16. Gregory Bateson, see Appendix.

17. E.E. Evans-Pritchard, see Appendix.

18. *The Andaman Islanders* (1922) by A.R. Radcliffe-Brown is an important early monograph based on fieldwork in 1906–8 in the Andaman Islands. https://bit.ly/33DjXog

19. W.J. Perry, see Appendix.

20. Grafton Elliot Smith, see Appendix.

21. Rumour of the disease's existence first circulated among US military personnel occupying post-World War II Japan in the late 1940s and later during the Korean War. The myth of Black Syphilis proliferated throughout the Asian world and among American military personnel during the Vietnam conflict, although strangely very few known *bona fide* cases have been medically documented.

22. 'Aryan' has its roots as a term used as a self-designation by Indo-Iranian people. The term was used by the Indo-Aryan people of the Vedic period in Ancient India as a religious label for themselves and as well as the geographic region known as Āryāvarta, where Indo-Aryan culture is based (in this region). https://en.wikipedia.org/wiki/Aryan

23. Alfred Haddon, see Appendix.

24. The Cambridge anthropological expedition of 1898–99 to the Torres Strait and New Guinea (the second expedition there) led by the zoologist

and anthropologist Alfred Cort Haddon (1855–1940), opened an epoch in field methodology. https://bit.ly/2GK7c2j

25. Of or pertaining to David Émile Durkheim (1858–1917) French positivist sociologist commonly cited as the principal architect of modern social science.

26. The sociological perspective, functionalism, developed from the writings of the French sociologist, Émile Durkheim (1858–1917). Durkheim argued that society was like a human body (the organic analogy). In order for society to run smoothly there has to be the correct balance of social cohesion and social control.

27. Patrick Geddes, see Appendix.

28. Leonard Hobhouse, see Appendix.

29. W.H.R. Rivers' 1920 book *Instinct and the Unconscious* attempts to put the system of psychotherapy into a biological setting, and explores at length the subconscious, repression, hysteria, neurosis, hypnotism, and many other related topics. Rivers (1864–1922) was an English neurologist, psychiatrist, and anthropologist. He is most famous for treating military personnel who suffered from shell shock during the First World War. https://amzn.to/33KhKaZ

30. *The Remembered Village* is a 1978 ethnological work by M.N. Srinivas. The book is about the small village, named as Rampura in the state of Karnataka, then called Mysore. It is notable for the absence of fieldnotes as a base for the work, which is considered standard in ethnography following the standards set by Bronislaw Malinowski in *Argonauts of the Western Pacific* as they were lost due to arson, and elicited fierce debate in the anthropological community due to its unorthodox origin, among other factors. The book is noted for its concern on the aesthetic, flowing prose and the significant role of the ethnographer himself, a marked departure from earlier works such as Evans-Pritchard's studies on the Nuer, which is written with a more objective voice. https://en.wikipedia.org/wiki/The_Remembered_Village

31. *The Fieldworker and the Field: Problems and Challenges in Sociological Investigation* by M.N. Srinivas, A.M. Shah and E.A. Ramaswamy was published in 1979 and it broke new ground in social investigation. Other research in the field has since been published, but the essays in this volume remain seminal texts. The 18 essays in the volume describe a variety of field research programmes within rural and urban India, in complex organisations and in contrasting societies from other parts of the world, including Japan, Sri Lanka and New Mexico. https://bit.ly/3iFK4zn

32. Community of women.

33. Palakkad is rightfully known as the Gateway of Kerala, giving the rest of India access to the State. Its other name is Palghat was contributed by British Raj. Palakkad is a land of palm trees and paddy fields. It's known to be rich in flora and fauna. https://palghat.net/

34. Nirmal Kumar Bose, see Appendix.

35. Kheda district is one of the 33 districts of Gujarat state in western India. Its central city, Kheda, is the administrative headquarters of the district. https://en.wikipedia.org/wiki/Kheda_district

36. Marcel Mauss, see Appendix.

37. André Béteille, see Part III, p.

38. Vokkaliga is a Hindu farming community with 54 sub-divisions in Karnataka. They have notable demographic, political, and economic dominance in the southern parts of Karnataka. https://en.wikipedia.org/wiki/Vokkaliga

39. The term Harijan literally means 'children of God'. It was a term first used by Mohandas Karamchand Gandhi to refer to Dalits in 1932. The exact origin of the word is, however, subject to debate. Dalit, meaning 'broken/scattered' in Sanskrit and Hindi, is a term used for people belonging to castes in India who have been subjected to untouchability. https://en.wikipedia.org/wiki/Dalit

40. Paul Radin, see Appendix.

41. Peter Berger, see Appendix.

42. Sacco and Vanzetti, see Appendix.

43. Anil Seal, see Appendix.

44. The Indian National Congress was founded in 1885. It was the first modern nationalist movement to emerge in the British Empire. From the late 19th century, and especially after 1920, under the leadership of Mahatma Gandhi, Congress became the principal leader of the Indian independence movement. Congress led India to independence from Great Britain, and powerfully influenced other anti-colonial nationalist movements in the British Empire. https://en.wikipedia.org/wiki/Indian_National_Congress

45. The Warlis or Varlis are an indigenous tribe or Adivasis, living in mountainous as well as coastal areas of Maharashtra-Gujarat border and surrounding areas. They have their own animistic beliefs, life, customs and traditions, as a result of acculturation they have adopted many Hindu beliefs. The Warlis speak an unwritten Varli language which belong to the southern zone of the Indo-Aryan languages. https://en.wikipedia.org/wiki/Warli

46. Thakkar Bapa, see Appendix.

47. Verrier Elwin, see Appendix.

48. Louis Dumont, see Appendix.

49. David Pocock, see Appendix.

50. Narayan Sheth, see Appendix.

51. In 1952, the Union Government decided that all cases pertaining to the allocation of grants-in-aid from public funds to the Central Universities and other Universities and Institutions of higher learning might be referred to the University Grants Commission. Consequently, the University Grants Commission (UGC) was formally inaugurated by late Shri Maulana Abul Kalam Azad, the then Minister of Education, Natural Resources and Scientific Research on 28 December 1953. The UGC, however, was formally established only in November 1956 as a statutory body of the Government of India through an Act of Parliament for the coordination, determination and maintenance of standards of university education in India. https://www.ugc.ac.in/page/Genesis.aspx

52. V.K.R.V. Rao, see Appendix.

53. Homi Bhabha, see Appendix.

54. The Khasi people are an indigenous ethnic group in Meghalaya in north-eastern India with a significant population in the bordering state of Assam, and in certain parts of Bangladesh. The Khasi form the majority of the population of the eastern part of Meghalaya, and is the state's largest community, with around 48 per cent of the population of Meghalaya. They are the only Mon-Khmer speaking people in South Asia. A cultural tradition of the Khasi people is that they follow the matrilineal system of descent and inheritance. https://en.wikipedia.org/wiki/Khasi_people

55. The Garos are an indigenous Tibeto-Burman ethnic group from the Indian subcontinent, notably found in the Indian states of Meghalaya, Assam, Tripura, Nagaland, and neighbouring areas of Bangladesh, notably Mymensingh, Netrokona, Jamalpur, Sherpur and Sylhet. Historically, Garo name was used for a wide range of people on the southern bank of the Brahmaputra. They are the second-largest tribe in Meghalaya after the Khasi and comprise about a third of the local population. The Garos are one of the few remaining matrilineal societies in the world. https://en.wikipedia.org/wiki/Garo_people

56. The Pnar, also known as Jaiñtia, are a sub-tribal group of the Khasi Tribe in Meghalaya, India. The Pnar people are matrilineal. They speak the Pnar language which belongs to the Austro-Asiatic language family and is very similar to the Khasi language. The Pnar people are natives of West

Jaintia Hills and East Jaintia Hills District of Meghalaya, India. https://en.wikipedia.org/wiki/Pnar_people

57. The Indian Council of Social Science Research (ICSSR) was established in the year of 1969 by the Government of India to promote research in social sciences in the country. ICSSR provide grants for projects, fellowships, international collaboration, capacity building, survey, publications etc. to promote research in social sciences in India. https://icssr.org/

PART three

André Béteille. Photograph courtesy Alan Macfarlane.

André Béteille

André Béteille (born 30 September 1934) is an Indian sociologist and writer. He is well known for his studies of the caste system in South India. He was a Professor of Sociology at the Delhi School of Economics at the University of Delhi where, since 2003, he remains Professor Emeritus of Sociology. He was appointed National Research Professor by the Government of India in 2007 Presently he is the Chancellor of North Eastern Hill University, Shillong, Meghalaya and prior to that he was the Chancellor of Ashoka University.

In his long and distinguished career, he has taught at Oxford University, Cambridge University, the University of Chicago and the London School of Economics, the Erasmus University of Rotterdam, the University of California at Berkeley, and the Institute of Advanced Study, Berlin.

A brilliant mind, Béteille, even at an early age, received numerous awards and fellowships from a number of universities both in India and abroad. He was the first Nehru Fellow. In 1992, in recognition of his scholarly contributions to the field of sociology, he was elected as a Corresponding Fellow of the British Academy – a distinction that rarely comes to an Indian and that too, to a sociologist.

In 2005, in recognition of his work in the field of sociology and his distinguished service to the nation, he was awarded the Padma Bhushan by the President of India. The same year he was appointed as a member of the Prime Minister's National Knowledge Commission which he quit in protest in 2006, following a proposal for increasing caste-based reservations. The same year, he was made National Professor, and is currently Chairman of the Centre for Studies in Social Sciences, Kolkata.

Béteille was born in the town of Chandannagore, the youngest of three brothers and a sister. He grew up in Bengal, spent a part of his school years and all his college and university days in Calcutta. He is equally comfortable with Bengali as in English. He has profound knowledge of European, particular English, literature, and is an accomplished singer of Rabindranath Tagore's songs, whenever he is away from his books.

His publications include Caste, Class and Power: Changing Patterns of Stratification in a Tanjore Village *(1965),* Castes: Old and New, Essays in Social Structure and Social Stratification *(1969),* Inequality and Social Change *(1972),* Studies in Agrarian Social Structure *(1974),* Six Essays in Comparative Sociology *(1974),* Inequality among Men *(1977),* The Idea of Natural Inequality and Other Essays *(1983), and* Society and Politics in India: Essays in a Comparative Perspective *(1991).*[1]

Alan Macfarlane (AM): It's a great pleasure to introduce this afternoon, Professor André Béteille, a professor of sociology at the University of Delhi and author of a number of distinguished works on Indian society and on general problems of human society. André, I'd like to ask you first something about your background and upbringing. Tell us something about your childhood and family background.

André Béteille (AB): Well, probably from the point of view of anthropology, the most important part of my background is that I was born in India and I grew up in India as the offspring of a mixed marriage. My mother was Indian, Bengali, and my father was French. Now he was born in India himself, but he was French-speaking and born of French parents in India and I grew up with a rather uncertain position between these two cultures, and well, I had a sort of middle-class education that many people who later became professionals would have had.

I was sent to a boarding school where I was taught English although the language I learnt and used at home as a child was neither French nor English but Bengali, but I was sent off to boarding school where I was taught to speak English. And then, went to college as an undergraduate in Calcutta. Actually, I'd started as a student of physics and after some time gave that up and took up anthropology. And initially I wasn't at all sure as to what I wanted to become, whether a social anthropologist or an archaeologist, or a physical anthropologist but gradually I moved into social anthropology and began teaching in the Department of Sociology in the University of Delhi,[2] so that although I work with anthropologists and I am regarded by many as an anthropologist, I actually work in the Department of Sociology in the University of Delhi.

This interview was conducted by Alan Macfarlane on 1 June 1986. The transcription for this interview was provided by Sanjeeb Mukherjea, for this volume.

These interviews are available for viewing on:
https://www.sms.cam.ac.uk/media/1113102
https://www.youtube.com/watch?v=dWKFnqfUDNY

AM: What first attracted you to read social anthropology, why were you interested in it?
AB: Well I suppose I had a kind of natural inclination if you can call it that, towards trying to compare and understand the ways of life of various kinds of people. I could see that there was such a contrast between the background from which my mother came and the one from which my father came. And that sort of created in me an interest in the diversity of human cultures and ways of life, and that I think was a very important factor in my orientation towards anthropology and the comparative study of human societies.

AM: Did you go and do a postdoctoral or a postgraduate degree in anthropology?
AB: Well, I did. I did an honours degree in anthropology from the University of Calcutta[3] and after that an M.Sc. in anthropology. The M.Sc. is a sort of taught degree and you take courses for two years and then then take exams at the end of it and you get an M.Sc. degree. It's not a research degree.

Shortly after that, a new Department of Sociology was opened in the University of Delhi which was then emerging as probably the premier university in the country and I moved to the University of Delhi as a lecturer in sociology. So I started teaching sociology and then I began my research for my PhD degree. And I was fortunate that this new department was headed by a very, very distinguished and a very remarkable person, the anthropologist M.N. Srinivas,[4] and I worked with him for my PhD, and I did this while I was while I was teaching sociology in the University of Delhi.

AM: We'll probably talk about those people later on, but since you've mentioned M.N. Srinivas, what sort of man was he and what sort of influence do you think he had on your own work?
AB: Oh I think he influenced my work very greatly but there was another influence on my work, from a man whom I had got to know in Calcutta, who was also an anthropologist and had been involved in the nationalist movement, a man called N.K. Bose.[5]

But in my professional training as an anthropologist I think the influence of Srinivas was very great. I think Srinivas was in many ways a very remarkable person. He had a very sensitive mind, he was very persuasive in conversation, he was not a great lecturer, and he wrote well, but I don't think that he had a great mind for formal theory.

But he could, he could convey to you the sense of the richness and the variety of any kind of social situation – the inherent richness and complexity in any kind of social situation. He used to say that 'you know, social life is untidy, it's very untidy and you mustn't try to tidy it up too much'. And I think that is very important. As a sociologist, I am inherently suspicious of theorists who try to make social reality appear more coherent than one normally experiences it as being.

AM: Was it Srinivas who made you particularly interested in caste or was that ....

AB: No, I don't think Srinivas had a line in that sense – if he had a line, it was fieldwork. He insisted that in order to understand society, 'you must go out and live with people, see what they're doing'. And this was a great departure in India not only in social theory in general, but in India which has had a very long intellectual tradition but one that has unfortunately paid very little attention to observation and description. It's an intellectual tradition which has had a pronounced preoccupation with formal theory.

And Srinivas sort of conveyed in all of us the importance of going out and seeing what was actually happening there. He always argued that 'there's a "book view" of society and a "field view" of society, and the two are not the same. And that you must learn this, and there's no way in which you can learn this just from books. You go out into the villages, you go and live in a village or live with the community and you will realize that the way it works is very different from the way in which it is supposed to work'. And I think that is very important.

AM: Was it he who suggested that you went to Tanjore,[6] or, how did you come to choose....

AB: More or less.... He was very, in many ways, he was very permissive. I mean he didn't insist on, at least with me, he didn't insist that I should do this particular thing or that particular thing. I think there was an idea at first that I would work with Tamil speakers in Delhi. And again this was rather unusual because in India, most people who made empirical studies, studied people in their own community or in their own linguistic region. And Srinivas you must remember, had been trained in Oxford by Radcliffe-Brown,[7] and he had a great admiration for Evans-Pritchard.[8] So he insisted I should work in an area which was very different from the one in which I had grown up.

Now, this was very unusual for social studies in India. I am Bengali speaking, I came from West Bengal in eastern India, so Srinivas said, 'you must choose some other community, you must learn a new language, you must come to terms with a different way of life from the one in which you have grown up'.

And at first there was an idea that I might study Tamil speakers in Delhi, a neighbourhood consisting of Tamil speakers in Delhi, but I thought that would be rather dull and I went off to Tanjore. I think the choice of Tanjore was mainly my own idea, and that time I was excited by the possibility of studying this part of India which had a very rich religious tradition, which had ancient temples, you know, the kind of thing that Chris Fuller[9] finally did; that was more the kind of thing I thought I would do when I was going out to Tanjore. But it turned out actually very differently.

AM: So you intended to study religion, and ritual and matters such as that?

AB: Not religion as such, temples. I thought that in getting to understand the way in which the temple worked, I would look at many things besides religion. I thought that I would look at politics, at economics, and not just religion and ritual. No, I don't think that was ever my primary interest.

AM: When you arrived in the village coming from an entirely different part of India, do you recall your first impressions, your first surprises or....

AB: Yes, very vividly, very vividly. I was struck as much by the differences as by the similarities and both were in many ways unexpected. Now this is an area in which a very different language is spoken from the ones which I had spoken – either Bengali which was my native language or Hindi which is the language spoken in Delhi where I had already started working in the University of Delhi. Tamil is a totally different language; I'd learnt a bit of Tamil before coming out. And what struck me – I was living with a group of Brahmins – and they had an elaborate ritual vocabulary, much of which was highly Sanskritized.

And of course, Bengali is the most Sanskritized among Indian languages. So I not only surprised myself but I also surprised the people with whom I lived by my natural understanding of their ritual vocabulary, much of which was in Sanskrit and Sanskritized Bengali was not all that different. So that was one thing.

The other thing was of course, my mother's family were very orthodox Brahmins until my mother's generation. And my maternal grandmother lived in many ways the life of a Brahmin widow – the kind of life that has disappeared more or less from the cities now, in Bengal. For instance she would not wear shoes as she would go every morning to bathe in the river – my childhood was in Chandannagore which was a French enclave about 20 miles north of Calcutta. And she would go every morning to bathe and she would come back in her wet clothes and I've forgotten all this or thought that I put all this behind me. But when I went to live in this village about 20 years afterwards I would see these Sri Vaishnava Brahmin[10] widows coming back from their morning bath in the River Kaveri and this immediately brought back to me such an important part of my childhood. So I was certainly discovering myself while I was doing my fieldwork and also discovering many things which were very different from what I'd expected them to be.

AM: Such as....

AB: Oh, such as for instance the relations between castes were much more rigid and formal than anything that I had experienced in the city of Calcutta or in the city of Delhi. For instance, the attention which these Brahmins paid to matters of detail not only in their religious life but in their ordinary everyday customs – like the way they ate their food, the kind of food they ate, the way they served their food, their dress and so on and so forth. All this struck me as such an elaborate and formalized world which was very different from the very fluid and amorphous world of the city of Calcutta where I had grown up and where I got to school and got to college. It was very different.

AM: Did you, like many anthropologists, find their first fieldwork particularly rather difficult through loneliness or sickness, or lost privacy or whatever? Did you find it to be a difficult experience?

AB: Yes, loss of privacy was something which worried me very much and that again is something worth noting because after all one might say that that an English or an American anthropologist might be worried by loss of privacy while doing fieldwork in an African tribe or an Indian village. But why should an Indian be worried about that – but the point is that I was, and I'm sure that there would be very many Indians in my position who would be worried by the loss of privacy there. And as one incident which remains in my memory, which struck me very much at that point of time, which has to do with loss of privacy. I'd rented the room upstairs in a house which was owned by an elderly Brahmin couple. And it was actually a large single room with a veranda in the front end and a terrace at the back. And I had a small camp bed and I would greatly look forward to an hour in the afternoon when I could go and sleep there because it was quite hot. And I used to do that.

Soon I found that there was a young man in the village who didn't have much to do – he would come with his mat, unroll it just below my camp bed and go to sleep. And I found this profoundly disturbing. So I took my problem to my patron in the village who was a college educated Brahmin landowner. I took my problem to him and said, 'Look I'm sorry I have a small problem'. He would ask me this every time we met, 'Are you all right are you comfortable do you have any problems' and I said, 'Well I have a small problem' and he said, 'Oh you must tell me what is it', and I said, 'You know it's this man Varadhan'. He said, 'Oh I know this fellow, is he troubling you'. I said, 'Well not really but you know'. He said, 'Well what does he do, is he asking you for money', I said, 'No', then 'What does he actually do?' I said, 'Well you know in the afternoon, I like to rest', and he said, 'Well he comes and badgers you?' And well I couldn't say that he did that because he didn't. I said, 'Well he comes and he sleeps there you know'. He said, 'Well does he snore?' and I couldn't say that he did because he didn't but then he said 'but what does he do', I said, 'Well', he looked at me and he said, 'But why does it worry you, why does it worry you?' And I felt that really, I mean he put it in such a way that it made me feel that I was in the wrong and I think that that was a very important lesson for me. That I was bothered by the lack of privacy. I can't say that I very greatly enjoy fieldwork – I certainly enjoy it in retrospect more than I possibly did while I was doing fieldwork and I'm not a great figure. I mean Srinivas was superb as a fieldworker I've had students who were very good fieldworkers, but I mean I'm sort of B– to B as a fieldworker.

AM: Whatever your views of yourself as a fieldworker, you wrote a thesis about this fieldwork and then you wrote a very widely used book *Caste, Class and Power*.[11] Could you say what the theme of that book is and what you found in your work?

AB: Yeah well, the book in fact was my PhD thesis. I mean I didn't spend very much time over the thesis, I made some changes and sent it off to the University of California Press and to my surprise they agreed to publish it. Well basically, the book was a village study. However you must remember that anthropology was changing its orientation in India. Until the fifties most anthropologists studied tribes. It was only in the fifties that village studies began to acquire the kind of importance that they had assumed when I started doing my work – so it was to be a village study that was clear.

Now what was I going to study in the village? Now there had already been a few village studies published. There was F.G. Bailey's[12] *Caste in the Economic Frontier*, Adrian Mayer's[13] book *Caste and Kinship in Central India*, and then this very widely used collection edited by McKim Marriott[14] – *Village India*[15] and it struck me that all these books had a kind of framework within which they described the social structure of what was going on in the village, and their framework was a sort of morphological framework in which the basic structure was the caste structure. In other words, they would give a presentation of the caste structure of the village and within that framework discuss whatever else they considered interesting.

Adrian Mayer wrote on kinship, Bailey wrote on economics and politics, somebody else worked on religion and so on. But I felt that this was a very important morphological feature of the village, it was there in the settlement pattern of the village. So you couldn't escape the caste structure. So I looked at the caste structure and the division of the village into Brahmins, non-Brahmins, untouchables and their sub-divisions and the way in which all this was arranged in a certain pattern. But I soon realized that there was something else also in the village which was perhaps as important, even though it didn't strike one as immediately. And that was the division of the village into land owners, tenants and landlords which I describe as the class system. I found that there was also a certain distribution of power in the village so I tried to describe first, each of these three structures, the caste structure——the division of the village into its various castes and their arrangement——then the class system, then the power structure and I could also see that the village was changing a great deal. And I thought that well, one might describe what changed by taking up each of these systems and describing changes in them in turn, or one might try to examine the relationship between caste, class and power and see how that relationship itself was changing. So this is basically the theme of the book. What was the nature of the relationship between caste, class and power at the end of the 19th century and towards the beginning of the 20th century – I found that there was a great deal of correspondence between these three systems so that the Brahmins were mainly the landowners and they occupied the commanding heights and the distribution of power and the non-Brahmins were the tenants and they occupied the middle levels of power and the untouchables were at the lowest end of the hierarchy.

AM: Did you find a correspondence and exact correspondence between the class, general dimensions of the class structure and the structure of power and class?

AB: Well yeah, I mean this is really what caught my attention. Of course there was a great deal of correspondence but this correspondence was changing. I could see that it was changing and I was interested in identifying the forces which brought about this change and that really was the theme of the book.

Fifty years before I did my fieldwork, most Brahmins were landlords and most landlords were Brahmins, and the Brahmin landlords also occupied the commanding heights in the power structure. But when I was doing my fieldwork – much of the land was still owned by the Brahmins, but there were many Brahmins who had lost their land and there were many more non-Brahmins by then who were landowners. But more important than that there had come about a quite striking dissociation between caste and power. Power had shifted from the hands of the Brahmins, and the non-Brahmins now controlled the institutions of power so the correspondence was far less clear now and apart from describing it, this growing dissociation first between caste and land ownership, and then between caste and power – I was interested in identifying the forces which were bringing this about. This is really the argument of the book, or the subject of the book.

AM: Looking back on the book which was written some years ago now are there any parts of it with which you are now particularly dissatisfied or felt that you would have written it in a different way if you were doing it now?

AB: Probably yes, I mean there are many obvious deficiencies in the book. I mean I ought to have presented far more data on the distribution of land than I did, and I ought to have collected far more data on that than I did. And probably I would have liked to do that but I think in a way I'm glad that I finished with the book and moved on to other things. Because if I dwelt too long with that kind of thing I might not have moved into the areas over which I sort of roamed the last twenty years or so——the book was published in 1965, twenty-one years now, and I don't regret the fact that the book might have been much better if I'd spent another five years over it because I did other things in those five years.

AM: One of the things you moved on to and which has been one of the central preoccupations of your academic life is the theme of equality and inequality in human societies. I was wondering first what do you think has made you so very interested in this area, maybe an obvious answer....

AB: Well, I mean there is a great deal of inequality in Indian society that one sees and one tries to understand it living in that society, but

I've always been struck by the fact that inequality is a very pervasive feature of all human societies.

My childhood was spent in a colonial system so I could see quite well that although Indians had lived with inequality for centuries and millennia I mean the Indians hadn't invented inequality. The colonial system, the imperial system was a highly unequal system. So here was a problem which could be studied from many points of view, it was almost an inexhaustible problem. But after doing my book on this one single village, I moved on to do other things and I took up caste and I pursued that problem for another three or four years. Caste seen not just in the context of a single village but in a larger context and I published a series of papers which were then brought together as a book called *Castes: Old and New*,[16] which dealt first with the changing status aspects of caste and the changing relations between caste and politics. And so I did that and then I moved on to the other dimension which I had discussed in my monograph, namely class. I spent a couple of years studying agrarian relations between landowners tenants landless labourers not just in a single village but in different parts of the country and it was only after that that I moved on to more general studies of inequality.

AM: If that's the chronological order then perhaps we should deal with the question of caste next. Did you find the work of Srinivas on Sanskritization[17] and on the mobility of the caste system helpful in your work?

AB: Yes it was very helpful but I think that it was very limited also. I think one of my——what I consider to be one of my most important papers——was an early essay on the Backward Classes that is the untouchables, tribals and the Other Backward Classes. It was written for a particular collection of studies which were projections of what things might be like 20 years or 25 years hence. It was called 'The Future of the Backward Classes – The Competing Demands of Status and Power'.

And I found that what was wrong with the idea of Sanskritization is that the inferior castes were now particularly after independence concerned not simply with improving their status with imitating their superiors and improving their status in that way but they were also concerned with engaging in political contests with them – in mobilizing political support on the basis of caste identities. And if they were doing that, then it might become important to assert their inferior status rather than to try to leave it behind. The kind of situation that you find with regard to Blacks in the United States – there's a whole history of attempts by blacks to pass which one might compare with Sanskritization. Then the political system acquires a certain character which encourages Blacks to turn around and assert their deprived or deprivileged status in order to make political gains. So I think that Sanskritization was important but there are other forces which act against Sanskritization and I felt that Srinivas hadn't looked sufficiently deeply at these.

AM: You talked about projecting into the future, have you any thoughts on the future of the caste system? It's a very large question but I know you've been thinking about this recently, whether it's going to develop as you suggested a little higher in to a system of political groupings based on ethnic supposed ethnic identities and castes or whether it's going to disappear as was once hoped or whether it will remain or change?

AB: I don't think it's going to disappear. I think that you know, shortly after independence Indians who had hoped a great deal from economic planning and parliamentary system, and that kind of thing, a scientific education, perhaps thought that caste might disappear in a generation or two. I don't think that is going to happen at all but I don't think that it's going to remain what it has been. It's changing in many important ways but I think that caste identities will continue to be a feature of Indian social structure for a very long time.

AM: Caste is obviously very closely related to Hinduism. A rather technical question but I wonder whether you would accept an account of Hinduism as a Durkheimian[18] status confirming religion grown to a sort of world sociological religion – in other words that caste is merely a reflection of a religious system and has nothing in itself, it's a system of ideas?

AB: Well no, I don't. I don't think I would agree with that although I see that the religious basis of caste played a very important part in keeping it in business for 2000 years. But I can easily see these collective identities outliving these religious beliefs and values by which they were sustained. I can quite easily see inferior castes asserting their collective identities as inferior castes, in the interest of securing greater political and other material advantages without necessarily subscribing to the orthodox Hindu theory of purity and pollution.

AM: So even without Hinduism, Hinduism faded, caste can continue?
AB: In principle yes, but I don't see either Hinduism or caste fading away, therefore it's a question to which I can't apply my mind very easily.

AM: You continued on this theme and moved on to questions of equality and inequality and you've often reflected on whether man is basically born equal or born unequal – questions which trace back obviously to Aristotle[19] and more recently to Rousseau.[20] Can you give a quick answer to the question of whether you think that man is essentially born equal or unequal?
AB: Well I don't put that question in that form. I mean, what I would say is that the conditions of collective life are such that it is inconceivable without at least two forms of inequality. The conditions of collective life require first of all a certain system of values and scales of evaluation which generate inequalities of status.

The conditions of collective life further require a certain kind of organization of activities; coordination and organization of activities which generate inequalities of power. So that I would rather say that you know I find it very difficult to conceive of human societies without any inequality at all. Because I find it very difficult to conceive of human societies which are not governed by some values on which people agree and values which rank persons, beings, things, objects on scales, and you have inequality as a consequence of that.

And I find it difficult to conceive of human societies which are not organized, at least minimally organized, with some inequalities in the distribution of power, some kind of chain of command and obedience are fine; difficult to conceive of societies otherwise.

AM: Would you accept, I mean that those are your own views, but would you accept that societies do have a general view of themselves and a premise about whether man is basically born equal or unequal and that this is one of the things that differentiates basically modern industrial individualistic Western societies from societies like India – the premise of equality in the West and the premise of inequality in India.

AB: Oh, I think that societies differ very much in what they consider to be the proper basis of collective life and there have been societies in the past which have considered hierarchy as a part of the natural scheme of things and from that point of view they're very different from modern societies which seek to build up collective life on the premise of equality so they are very different from each other. But I would just say that you know, I mean yeah, I know that there'd be sharp disagreement on this – I would say really that the basic difference there is not so much between India and the West as between the past and the present. I think that Indian society today in many important ways views itself or views its own ideal as being a society which is based on the premise of equality.

AM: And the past would be for India when – the turning point?

AB: Yeah, the past was much longer in the case of India, much longer than in the case of the West certainly – 19th century, I would say in the 19th century was the turning point.

AM: And in the West? I know you were meant to be a historian...

AB: Certainly, I mean certainly it's well on its way by the time the Industrial Revolution[21] comes and I mean the West is not one undifferentiated unit certainly and——but you know I mean this—— this image is all very well. I find that even in the United States today which is probably one society which has gone further than other Western industrial societies in its faith in equality; the American creed so-called, I think, that people would argue that some inequalities are not only necessary but perhaps also desirable.

I mean I think the most striking thing about the attitude of contemporary societies to equality is that it is an ambivalent attitude. These societies very strongly want equality of opportunity but I'm not quite sure that they want equally strongly equality of outcome, equality of result or equal distribution of benefits. So these societies are very strongly achievement-oriented – and if you place a very high value on individual achievement what does it mean? It simply means that some individuals achieve more than others even though you insist that the conditions of their competition should be equalized.

AM: Do you think a real belief in an afterlife which differentiates between the sinners and the saved helps to overcome the observed inequalities in this life?
AB: Yes I think so.

AM: In the absence of this, the general belief in Christianity, for example, means that the injustice, apparent injustice of the inequalities as observed around you if you have the premise of equality means that there's a psychic or psychological burden for people to understand how this could be…
AB: Yes indeed. And that is why these inequalities in modern societies are inherently unstable. They're inherently unstable because you have to correct them here and now; there is no other life in which they can be corrected. Yes, certainly. I mean I remember there's one of my favourite arguments and this is an observation made in one of Dostoevsky's[22] novels – in *The Brothers Karamazov*,[23] in which Ivan says 'if there is no immortality there is no virtue'. And I think that is very important.

AM: Does Hinduism overcome this problem? Like there are offences here you may not get to be punished here, but there will be some evening out in the end.
AB: Yeah well, this is a point that I'd like to stress – Hinduism may overcome this problem. I cannot really say because I'm not a Hindu. Hinduism may overcome this problem but Hindus don't seem to be able to overcome it in the modern world.

AM: The person with whom many of us have grown up in discussing these sorts of general problems is Louis Dumont[24] and I know that you have worked with him and battled with him. Perhaps you could just summarize what you think his main argument is and then comment on it.

AB: Well I mean, let me say that I've found myself embattled with two kinds of theories. One is the sort of materialist interpretation of history. Marxism[25] may not be a very great force in social anthropology but it is an important intellectual force in India and I found myself embattled with Marxism – a kind of Marxism which seeks to explain everything in terms of the economic base or the material structure of society, and to provide a complete explanation of social life and of history in terms of material forces.

And I have found myself embattled, equally strongly, against the opposite tendency which seeks to explain everything in terms of ideas, beliefs and values. So when you say that I have been embattled with Dumont, I would agree with that. But I would like to add that I find either kind of extreme position very difficult to accept.

I think that let me say what I consider to be unsatisfactory in Dumont's work – the first thing is that it is a definition of the sociology of India as being the sociology of Hinduism. I don't think that's a correct definition of the problem of understanding Indian society. Hinduism is a very important part of Indian society including contemporary Indian society but it's not the whole of Indian society, not the whole of contemporary Indian society, I think it pays far too little attention to economic and political forces operating in contemporary India.

AM: André, were there any other reasons why you felt that Dumont's work on India and caste was unsatisfactory.

AB: Well yes there's a second reason which I think is closely related to the first and probably it's a different way of stating the same criticism. I think that for Dumont, a preoccupation with ideas is what stands out as the defining feature of his work, and it's as if the sociology of ideas were the whole of sociology. I think he pays very little attention to a sociology of interests. For me a more adequate picture of Indian society would be one which incorporated a sociology of interests along with the sociology of ideas. I think I find Dumont's position too idealistic just as I find the position of my Marxist friends too materialistic. I think it's the interaction between ideas and interests which for me constitutes the essence of sociology.

AM: You are swiping out in both directions – to your left and to your right – and you mentioned to your right with Dumont to your left have you anything further to say on the Marxist, why you find a Marxist interpretation of Indian society unsatisfactory?
AB: Well I mean Marxism of course is a far bigger thing than Louis Dumont – I mean it's the whole enterprise, it's a whole intellectual and political enterprise. I think that Marxism engages me to a far greater extent than just the work of Louis Dumont because, first of all you have a much wider range of intellectual expressions of Marxism. Marxism would include on the one hand Lenin[26] and Bukharin,[27] and on the other hand Gramsci,[28] Lukacs[29] and the whole range of writers whose views, ideas on societies, on class would be very different from each other. And secondly I think that Marxism is very important not just in the battle of ideas it's very important in politics——in in——the struggle for power. And yes, I mean what I find unsatisfactory about Marxism is that it's very holistic – I mean it claims too much for a particular point of view and a particular approach, which is exactly why I find Dumont's kind of idealism unsatisfactory.

AM: You use the word holistic there – are you using it in the same sense of the distinction that Dumont makes between holistic and individualistic societies because really this is to ask you whether you feel that that distinction rather than the hierarchical and non-hierarchical distinction that he made is any more helpful in understanding?
AB: No, I think I'm using the word holistic in a rather loose sense. Let me explain the sense in which I'm using it. I mean I remember reading something by Bertrand Russell[30] when I was an undergraduate which has stuck very much in my mind, that he at some point, he says that 'academic philosophers since the time of Parmenides[31] have believed that the world is a unity. It is my most fundamental belief that this is absolute nonsense'. I think it's this point of view that you have a unified theoretical system whether based on the materialist interpretation of history or the primacy of ideas. It's this that I find very difficult to accept as a sociologist. If I'd been a theologian of course I would have revelled in that kind of thing but I think that sociology is very different from theology.

AM: It comes back to Srinivas' 'world not being too tidy'?
AB: Absolutely, precisely.

AM: But reverting to holism and individualism in a different sense, do you find the contrast Dumont makes between Western or as you might put it, modern societies which are individualistic and traditional, which might be Eastern societies which are holistic, helpful and....
AB: Yes, yes, certainly. But it depends on how far you push that distinction, it depends on whether you have an open attitude towards the contrast or take a dogmatic view of that contrast. Certainly I would agree that collective identities play a far more important part in some societies than in others.

I think, I mean Nehru who was India's first prime minister and also was a very remarkable writer put it somewhere in one of his books about Indian society; he says that 'in this society it's the family, the caste and the village that counts for everything, the individual counts for nothing'.

I mean this is the same idea really that Dumont is putting forward and I think that there's something to it, but I don't think that one should push it too far. Because I think that even in modern societies collective identities have shown a remarkable durability.

Take the United States for instance; the Black identity, the Jewish identity, ethnic identities of various kinds——take the case of Netherlands for instance——a country in which after all if individualism developed anywhere, I mean the Netherlands will be a very good example. But collective identities have shown remarkable persistence in the Netherlands.

So by saying this I don't mean to say that there's no case for making a contrast between modern societies which assigned far more importance to the individual, and all other societies. Because modern societies also have collective identities and other societies also assign some importance to the individual. I think that there is a genuine contrast but one must be careful not to push it too far.

AM: Dumont, just to refer to him for the last time, has obviously had a great influence on studies in India after his work. What do you think is the most important general questions on the agenda for work in India?

AB: Well I think, I mean, let me make this very clear – I think that Dumont's work has been very important and I think that it's a remarkable achievement. But I think that I'm uncomfortable with the almost exclusive emphasis that Dumont assigns to ideas.

I think I would like to see a greater emphasis assigned to material factors in the understanding of Indian society. I'd put it like this – that if I were to draw up an agenda for Indian sociology, I would put at the centre of that agenda the study of institutions, the study of organizations, the study of social action; rather than the study of ideas. And I think that there's a great deal to be done in that direction. I think that in one way or another, the sociology of Dumont has shifted attention away from the 'field view' of Indian society, to the 'book view' of Indian society, and I think that the time has now come for the balance to be redressed.

I mean, I don't think that the 'book view' we can ever afford to dispense with; the 'book view' of Indian society, no matter how greatly enthused we may be about fieldwork, but I think one has gone too far in the direction of the 'book view'.

AM: I wanted to ask you André one or two questions which now place India in comparison to some of the other major world religions in civilizations and starting with Islam. India or Hinduism particularly is based on the oppositions of purity and a hierarchical model as Islam to a certain extent is based on honour and violent conflict. Do you have any explanation why you have this difference?

AB: No, but I'm, you know as a sociologist, I'm less interested, in trying to work out the sources of these distinctions, than in their implications; what consequences does this distinction have for society or for economy, for politics, and I think that is something on which one might say a great deal. I mean the contrast between Islam and Hinduism has often been made in terms of contrast between equality and hierarchy.

I think that's valid up to a point, there's no doubt about that but once again I think one mustn't push too far the commitment to equality in actually existing Islamic societies. I mean, we have lived with an Islamic society for several hundred years and the court culture built up in the city in which I now live by the Mughals was certainly not an egalitarian culture in any sense of the term, it was a very hierarchical culture. Nevertheless, there is that difference between Islam and Hinduism, but I think that from the point of view of the contemporary world and contemporary politics, there's another difference which is very important.

I think that Hinduism has been in some sense a genuinely pluralistic religion which has not only tolerated, but in some sense encouraged diverse ways of life, diverse beliefs, diverse practices, and Islam has a deep core of fundamentalism in it. I made a contrast earlier between theology and sociology – I think from that point of view, I would say that Islam is more conducive to theology and less conducive to sociology, whereas I think that there's something to be said about the Hindu intellectual tradition being more in tune with what I would regard as a proper sociological perspective. I'd like to assert this – I say this not as a Hindu because I'm not a Hindu myself, but I think that there is something very important in the Indian intellectual tradition there.

AM: Another contrast one may make between two great civilizations is between India and China. It's difficult to point in time to make this but given a roughly similar geographical base and to a certain extent, similar environmental conditions, are there any easy answers to the question of why India seems so politically fragmented whereas China has a certain degree of integration at least at present, you think this is a long term trend or....

AB: It probably is a long term trend, I mean that's one contrast that China has been far more successful in managing its polity so to say than India – administrative structure of state apparatus and so on, but there is another contrast and I wonder whether the two contrasts are related to each other.

India has generated a very large number of religions. I mean if you look at India, it has been a cradle of so many major religions – Hinduism, Buddhism, Jainism and so on and so forth; and China has produced very little of that and I wonder whether India's weakness in generating a stable, coherent political order may not be linked with a proliferation of religious ideas, religious doctrines, religious views, and the opposite kind of correlation in China. But you know, I mean these are just very speculative suggestions I would say.

AM: Sounds like a remark about Switzerland which is so efficient and organized and coherent and integrated and so on and then it always ends with, well what has Switzerland produced – the cuckoo clock....The last contrast I was going to ask you to make – many people may have read Nirad Chaudhuri's[32] works and particularly, his reflections on the differences between England and India and his *Passage to England* and so on. As an Indian from Delhi coming to Europe what are your main——what gives you the most surprise when you come here, in terms of what you find as a culture in your looking as an anthropologist from the outside?

AB: Well I mean, you know, there are many surprises where I've described these as situational surprises rather than structural surprises. In the sense that I don't know how many lessons I would draw from these surprises, because you mustn't forget that England or Western Europe, and especially England has been a part of the sensibility of the modern educated Indian to a far greater extent than the opposite. And so, I mean I wouldn't expect any major surprises but of course there are differences and contrasts. I mean I think that the most striking contrast would be in the sphere of work and occupational rules, and the commitment to these occupational rules, and to work in general which is far better established throughout Western Europe than in India or in any South Asian country.

And conversely, the commitment to family, kinship, community is far more extensive in countries like India in that kind of society. But apart from that it would have to be very specific kinds of contrast you know. One would have to consider the fact that India is a highly differentiated society, highly stratified society, and so on.

AM: Well, most recently some of your work has been devoted to the question of the future of the Scheduled Tribes and Scheduled Castes[33] and I wanted particularly in relation to Scheduled Tribes – what you foresee the future of the remaining tribal groups in India?

AB: I think that these groups will remain. I mean, they will retain their distinctive identities at least for another two or three generations and it's very difficult for any sociologist to make any predictions beyond that. I just don't see them losing their distinctive identities, certainly not their language, certainly not their major social customs although more and more individual members of these tribal communities will become community-free in the sense that they will become incorporated into the modern occupational system and increasingly there will be areas of life in which their tribe or their community ceases to be relevant. But there will be other areas of life, for instance marriage, religious customs, in which they will continue to act as members of these particular tribes, but how rapidly this will happen and how extensively for the various tribes in the country, is very difficult to predict. Much will depend on the pace of economic change, development of education and so on.

AM: Could we turn now to one or two of the encounters you've had with people on your various visits to the West and their work. Perhaps to start with, any of your Indian colleagues you'd like to say anything more about – you mentioned Bose?

AB: Yes, well, I think I would, because he was——for two reasons I'd like to say something about him——firstly because he was in every respect a very remarkable person and secondly because his work is so little known outside India. He was a remarkable person because he did outstanding work as an anthropologist, but he was much more than an anthropologist.

He belonged to that generation of Indian intellectuals who were actively involved in the nationalist movement, and he had a tremendous range of interests. In fact, he published a book in the 1940s, a book which was published in Bengali and which I translated and published in English in the 1970s called *The Structure of Hindu Society* and that book in fact foreshadows many of the basic arguments that you find in the work of Dumont and Pocock.[34]

The book really is in three parts——the argument is——I mean he was a great fieldworker, he travelled throughout the country, lived with tribal people, studied fairs and pilgrim centres, and all the rest of it, and he constructed, he showed, that you could construct a certain picture of India, particularly its tribal people on the basis of ethnographic observation and description.

He showed that you could also construct a certain picture of Indian society particularly its tribal people on the basis of Indological study – a study of classical texts, and he showed the congruence between these two pictures – the idea that you get of Indian society by doing anthropological fieldwork and the idea that you get of Indian society by looking at the classical texts in fact confirm each other, they confirm a picture of a particular kind of structure. But then he went on to argue that that social structure was being dislocated from the middle of the 19th century onwards as India became involved more and more in a world economic system, in larger political conflicts and so on and so forth. So he was, I think a very remarkable person and has had a very great influence on being.

AM: André what would you think were the main contrasts in temperament and personality and academic style between Bose and Srinivas?

AB: Srinivas was a very mild-mannered and a very charming person, very relaxed sort of person who immediately put you at ease, he wasn't a very powerful speaker. Bose gave the impression, the immediate impression, of a magnetic personality someone who held your attention immediately.

Bose was in his element in an argument in a debate. Srinivas was a much more persuasive person, I mean he would try to persuade you and he would not try to impose an argument or a conclusion on you and Bose had in that sense arguments and conclusions which he felt ought to be categorically asserted. He was a very categorical person although a very rich mind and a very exciting person intellectually. Bose was a nationalist in a sense in which Srinivas was not.

Bose had been actively concerned with the National Movement and he believed that Indians ought to be more self-reliant in, in building up an apparatus for the study of their own society, he believed that there was a very rich intellectual tradition in India and you needed to tap that – mind you he was not an obscurantist in any sense but he felt very passionately about building up sociology in India through the effort of Indian intellectuals. I mean Srinivas was much more relaxed about that kind of thing.

Bose was trained entirely in India he never had been abroad till he was in his late 50s where Srinivas had been in Oxford, he'd been trained by Radcliffe-Brown and Evans-Pritchard and he was much more cosmopolitan. Srinivas was a much more cosmopolitan person in that sense.

AM: You have met and encountered very many of the European and American anthropologists in your various visits to the West and when they visited India. I wondered particularly the people who influenced you or you got to know well among them might be for example Max Gluckman[35] in Manchester. Could you say anything about it?

AB: Let me say very quickly, very briefly mention the people who have influenced me most among British anthropologists. Although I didn't have any close personal relationship with him, I think the person who influenced me most would be Evans-Pritchard. Although I met him once very briefly but he influenced me through his writings, and also through the influence he had on M.N. Srinivas who was very closely associated with him, and through the influence he had on various other people including Max Gluckman.

I knew Gluckman, I knew him, knew him fairly closely and really admired his work, and really appreciated his personal interest in me. He invited me over to Manchester the year after I'd finished my PhD, he invited me over to spend a year at Manchester as a Simon Fellow and I benefited very greatly by my contact with him. And it was in that year that I first made the acquaintance of Edmund Leach. And I would say that of that generation of anthropologists, these are the two people I got to know most closely and these are the two people with whom I have interacted most closely.

In some ways they're very unlike each other. You know there's a chapter in Adam Kuper's[36] book on British anthropology devoted to these two and he's called them 'two leading mavericks',[37] and I think that's very unfortunate because Max Gluckman was in no sense a maverick – he took his anthropology terribly seriously. He was very earnest about his anthropology. He was not a very tactful person always, but he was a very charismatic person and he took his anthropology very seriously. I don't think that I would say that of Edmund Leach[38] although I think that in his own way he's also been a tremendous intellectual force in British anthropology....

AM: And what would you think that Gluckman's main contribution to anthropology to be...what has been his intellectual contribution?

AB: I think in the same line as Srinivas I think that you know my way of looking at human societies is that you have to consider ideas beliefs and values, they are very important and they are autonomous up to a point. But you also have to consider interests and the conflict of interests and they too are autonomous up to a point. And what is really important in the study of any society is the interaction between ideas, beliefs and values on the one side and material interests on the other side.

I think that Gluckman's work was animated by this concern for the interplay between the two and I think that I got a great deal out of that. I mean Gluckman wrote a textbook of anthropology which he calls *Politics, Law and Ritual in Tribal Societies*,[39] and I think that's my idea of what social anthropology and sociology ought to be about, rather than working out the coherence of idea systems in themselves.

And Gluckman had a tremendous interest in fieldwork, in seeing how societies actually functioned, and you know, he developed this method of extended case studies. And there were a whole lot of people there, working in Manchester, it was John Barnes[40] whom I met in Manchester. John Barnes was in fact the first Simon Fellow in Manchester, then there was Clyde Mitchell[41] who had also been a Simon fellow in Manchester. And John Barnes had developed this idea about social networks as you know. And I wrote a paper which I published along with M.N. Srinivas, in fact it was a paper jointly published in *Man*[42] on social networks. Again I mean, Gluckman conveyed this sense of the complexity and the richness of human societies which are far more complex and rich than any theory can adequately represent.

AM: He was known not to be always on the best of terms with Sir Edmund Leach and so obviously there was a certain delicacy in the fact that you became friends with both of them, but turning to

Leach, in what ways do you feel he's influenced your work and do you admire his work?

AB: I greatly admire his work, but I mean Gluckman was, as I said, extremely earnest about his anthropology. Every Saturday he used to go with the whole Department to see a football match, and he was very earnest about that as well. Whereas Edmund Leach has always struck me as being very irreverent, very.

I remember very vividly my first encounter with Edmund Leach. I mean I knew a great deal about the folklore of British anthropology and I was very young then. He had invited me to lunch, and he used to share rooms in King's, this was before he became Provost of King's.

He had asked me over and I came about half an hour before lunch and he offered me a sherry and I drank the sherry and I was a bit awkward and stiff. So he offered me another glass of sherry and said, 'Oh come on have another', and I was hesitant and he's like, 'Oh come on, come on, have it', and then after that he offered me a third glass and I was really very hesitant and he laughed and said 'oh come on have it, I mean don't worry it's very good sherry and besides it's Meyer's sherry, not mine'.

I think that that was so characteristic of Edmund but apart from that, as an anthropologist, I think he had tremendous force and vitality. When I started teaching in the University of Delhi, as what – 23 or 24 years old and Srinivas gave me the syllabus and said that I would have to teach the course on political sociology, I had to read all those books because I hadn't. My training in Calcutta had been rather different from that and there were, I think half a dozen books which had to be explained very thoroughly to the students and which I had to read and some of those I hadn't read before and one of them was *Political Systems of Highland Burma*, and I think it is an absolutely superb book, one of the classics of modern anthropology.

AM: Edmund obviously had a great influence both in that book and in his latest work and his short-term or medium-term conversion to French structuralism. Can you assess his general contribution to the anthropology of the second half of this century or to British anthropology? Do you think is it now possible to place him in a way?

AB: Yes I think he shook British anthropology out of its complacency. I think there was a period in the development of anthropology when British anthropology was not only very strong, and very successful, but also somewhat complacent and I think Edmund Leach played a very important part in shaking this all up. I think what strikes me most about Edmund Leach is that although he was such a powerful intellectual figure, I think I'm right in saying that he studiously avoided the role of a *guru*.[43]

I think he was not interested in building up an intellectual school which he would then have to defend, and I said that for me, anthropology means equal attention to ideas and interests. And you see this in Edmund Leach's work, although in a very different way from the way in which you see it in Gluckman's work, or in Evans-Pritchard's work. You see it in Leach's work because I mean how does he define structure in the *Political Systems of Highland Burma*, it's basically a system of ideas. But then you see *Pul Eliya*[44] swings almost to the opposite extreme and I think the interesting thing about Leach is that he's never afraid to ask really important questions and when he doesn't find an answer to them, I think he admits that he hasn't found the answer and I think that's a remarkable quality.

AM: He obviously did manage to find sherry, though it would belong to Meyer Fortes![45] Another person you must have got to know and been influenced by was Meyer Fortes. What sort of man was he?

AB: Well I came to know Meyer Fortes rather late. I mean I knew his work of course, I mean we had to teach all that, because in the first ten years in the Department of Sociology at Delhi University, Srinivas was the dominant figure. And he had soaked up all this in his Oxford days and for Srinivas, sociology meant Radcliffe-Brown, Evans-Pritchard, Meyer Fortes.... So I knew his work but I didn't know him personally at all until I came to Cambridge in '78–'79, the year I spent here, and I got to know him.

What struck me most about Meyer Fortes is that he was a craftsman – he was really a craftsman who was prepared to go on for years on end, hammering out little bits and pieces and trying to put them into place, and I think that's very impressive.

As you know, he's written this autobiographical piece in which he divides anthropologists into pontiffs and journeymen, and I think that's very impressive; really the way in which he describes his own vocation, and I think he lived up to it and I think that's extremely impressive.

AM: Turning to – finally – one or two more general questions again and you've talked often interchangeably about sociology and anthropology. You are a professor of sociology and though you are known as an anthropologist as well. Do you see any opposition between these two disciplines or differences between them?

AB: Well, yes and no. You know I mean when I first started teaching sociology in the University of Delhi it was a big department it was an important department. We had to face criticism from our colleagues in other departments of sociology who were saying that what we were doing was not sociology at all but anthropology. And I argued in my lectures and in my writings for the unity of sociology and social anthropology – I argued that sociology and social anthropology were basically two different names for the same intellectual enterprise which is comparative sociology. And I think that——that I would still stand by that argument provided you defined anthropology as social anthropology in the way in which it was done by Radcliffe-Brown, Evans-Pritchard, Fortes, Gluckman.

But you know anthropology itself has changed a great deal. When I started my career in the late fifties, Radcliffe-Brown was a very important influence in anthropology. He was a very important figure in anthropology. But in the 1980s perhaps the most important figure in anthropology is Lévi-Strauss. And if I define anthropology as what Lévi-Strauss does, then I'm less confident about the unity of anthropology and sociology. This is because Lévi-Strauss himself has taken great pains in many of his writings to distinguish between the two. After all, what is anthropology – anthropology is *Le regard éloigné* (*The View From Afar*).[46] I can't honestly say when I'm studying Indian society that I'm taking a view from afar. So if that is what anthropology is then I'm not an anthropologist when I am studying Indian society. But I hope that's not the last word about anthropology.

AM: I hope not. Could I ask you just to come back to a topic we briefly discussed which is the question of nationalism and specifically the integration of the very many small groups in Indian society – the tribes and the castes, and the use of their identities. Do you see the future of India as a building contradiction between the centre and the periphery and these small subgroups which will more and more assert their separate identities, or do you think there is some possibility of a melting pot and unification?

AB: Well you know, I mean, it needn't be a melting pot. I mean you can have integration without these identities being dissolved. I mean you can have a pluralist political system in which these identities remain within a larger national whole. I would rather say that they are tensions, rather than contradictions; because tensions certainly there are, and I mean Indians themselves are very greatly preoccupied with what they describe as the problem of national integration – how to hold the nation together. And the threat of sub-nationalism has been a very important pre-occupation with Indians, and rather than tribes and castes I would say that the main threats to national integration are the identities which arise out of language and religion.

I mean tribe and caste over there, but regional identities which are mixed up with linguistic identities, they are an important threat to national integration. There's a form of sub-nationalism which threatens the larger national whole. Religious identity is also – I mean the country was once divided on the basis of religious identities and sometimes when the linguistic identity and the religious identity converge, then of course the threat becomes very large, as in the case of the Sikhs in the Punjab today. So that is certainly there but whether the country will hold together or break apart, I really don't know. All I can say is that I very much hope that it will hold together, there's no reason why it should not really.

AM: Finally André, although you're in a series of interviews with many great men who have achieved major work, you are in fact in the middle of your work, I was wondering what are your own plans for the next year or two and what you're working on and what next——in the sense in your own work——what are you most interested in pursuing next?

AB: Well as you remember, I was here in Cambridge last year, almost exactly this time last year, to give the Smuts Lectures which were on the theme of positive discrimination and social justice. And there were four lectures basically on the backward classes in India, their position in contemporary Indian society and the problem of creating special opportunities for them without violating the general principle of equal opportunities for all and this is something that I hope to pursue and perhaps write up as a bigger work on an important aspect of Indian society, the structure of Indian society.

AM: Well, I think I would like to thank you very much indeed André for a fascinating insight into the problems of being a comparative sociologist bridging many cultures, many traditions. Thank you very much and I look forward to another interview like this in about 10 years' time.

AB: Thank you.

NOTES

1. Your Article Library. 2020. https://bit.ly/2GyBSEa

2. The Department of Sociology was established by the University of Delhi in 1959 as a constituent of the Delhi School of Economics with the eminent sociologist Professor M.N. Srinivas as Head of the Department. To begin with, the Department trained students for two courses: M.A. and PhD In 1966, a two-year course for the M. Litt. degree was introduced. This has been replaced since 1976 by an M. Phil. degree course of a year's duration. In 1968, the Department was recognized as a Centre of Advanced Study in Sociology by the University Grants Commission (UGC), the first Department of Sociology to receive this recognition and has continued to be a Centre of Advanced Study since then. http://sociology.du.ac.in/history/

3. The Court of Directors of the East India Company sent a despatch in July 1854 to the Governor-General of India in Council, suggesting the establishment of the Universities of Calcutta, Madras and Bombay. In pursuance of that despatch, the University of Calcutta was founded on 24 January 1857. https://www.caluniv.ac.in/about/Foundation.html

4. M.N. Srinivas, see Part II, p. 51.

5. N.K. Bose, see Appendix.

6. Thanjavur, formerly Tanjore, city, eastern Tamil Nadu state, southeastern India. It lies in the Kaveri (Cauvery) River delta, about 30 miles (50 km) east of Tiruchchirappalli. https://www.britannica.com/place/Thanjavur-India

7. A.R. Radcliffe-Brown, see Appendix.

8. E.E. Evans-Pritchard, see Appendix.

9. Chris Fuller, see Appendix.

10. The Sathatha Sri Vaishnavas, also known as Chattada Sri Vaishnavas or Sattada Sri Vaishnavas, are a caste living throughout the Indian states of Andhra Pradesh, Karnataka, Tamil Nadu and Telangana. For several centuries, they have rendered a variety of services in Sri Vaishnava temples as *archakas*, *dharmakartas*, *progithar*, guardians of temple properties and suppliers of flowers such as garlands for worship. https://en.wikipedia.org/wiki/Sathatha_Sri_Vaishnava

11. *Caste, Class and Power* is an intensive study of the changing patterns of social stratification in a multi-caste village in South India. This village provides the background for this unusual description of contemporary change in a traditional society reacting to outside pressures. The transformation in the village takes the direction of a more open social system. Previously, village social life was shaped by its division into three caste groups: the Brahmins, the middle-level Non-Brahmins, and the Adi-Dravidas. The caste of a villager determined his position in the class system and power hierarchy, and caste itself was acquired only by birth. Professor Béteille shows how new forces are disrupting the existing pattern and producing economic and political systems that no longer depend entirely on caste. He concludes that the caste structure, once the basis of traditional order, does not afford an adequate framework for the analysis of Indian village society today. The author seeks to provide a more differentiated analytical scheme for the study of social change in India. This, the second, edition has additional matter on the genre of village studies: a retrospective of the author's experiences, and a review of the different ways in which caste and class have been studied. It also examines the role of temples in social organisation. The book ends with the author's description of fieldwork in this village. https://bit.ly/2GIa28r

12. Frederick George Bailey, see Appendix.

13. Adrian Mayer, see Part I, p. 9.

14. McKim Marriott, see Appendix.

15. Marriott's edited *Village India: Studies in the Little Community* (1955) is one of the most well-known collections of village studies in

the fifties, and even today it could be considered eminently relevant. It includes contributions by both foreign and Indian anthropologists. https://bit.ly/2GN3tRB

16. There is still debate in India as to whether caste is growing more or less important in modern social and political life, even though social inequalities based on caste are much less important now than 50 years ago. Nevertheless new kinds of gradations are appearing in Indian society; whether or not the word 'caste' can be applied to this phenomenon is largely a question of terminology. This analysis is primarily concerned with the changing status of Indian social groups and it presents, in the form of a series of essays, distinctive features of Indian society at present, based on income, occupation, education and living standards of the Harijans, Adivasis, the middle classes and the elite. https://www.cabdirect.org/cabdirect/abstract/19701801096

17. Sanskritization was a term introduced by M.N. Srinivas to Indian sociology in the 1950s. It refers to a process wherein a low caste, tribe or other groups collectively change their customs, rituals, ideology and way of life in the direction of some upper dominant caste to acquire higher status in the society. https://www.rajras.in/sanskritization/

18. Of or pertaining to Émile Durkheim (1858–1917) French positivist sociologist commonly cited as the principal architect of modern social science.

19. Aristotle, see Appendix.

20. Rousseau, see Appendix.

21. Industrial Revolution, in modern history, the process of change from an agrarian and handicraft economy to one dominated by industry and machine manufacturing. This process began in Britain in the 18th century and from there spread to other parts of the world. https://www.britannica.com/event/Industrial-Revolution

22. Dostoevsky, see Appendix.

23. *The Brothers Karamazov* is a murder mystery, a courtroom drama, and an exploration of erotic rivalry in a series of triangular love affairs involving the 'wicked and sentimental' Fyodor Pavlovich Karamazov and his three sons – the impulsive and sensual Dmitri, the coldly rational Ivan, and the healthy, red-cheeked young novice Alyosha. Through the gripping events of their story, Dostoevsky portrays the whole of Russian life, is social and spiritual striving, in what was both the golden age and a tragic turning point in Russian culture. https://www.goodreads.com/book/show/4934.The_Brothers_Karamazov

24. Louis Dumont, see Appendix.

25. Marxism is a social, political, and economic philosophy named after Karl Marx, which examines the effect of capitalism on labour, productivity, and economic development and argues for a worker revolution to overturn capitalism in favour of communism. Marxism posits that the struggle between social classes, specifically between the bourgeoisie, or capitalists, and the proletariat, or workers, defines economic relations in a capitalist economy and will inevitably lead to revolutionary communism. https://www.investopedia.com/terms/m/marxism.asp

26. Lenin, see Appendix.

27. Bukharin, see Appendix.

28. Antonio Gramsci, see Appendix.

29. Georg Lukács, see Appendix.

30. Bertrand Russell, see Appendix.

31. Parmenides of Elea, active in the earlier part of the 5th c. BCE, authored a difficult metaphysical poem that has earned him a reputation as early Greek philosophy's most profound and challenging thinker. His philosophical stance has typically been understood as at once extremely paradoxical and yet crucial for the broader development of Greek natural philosophy and metaphysics. https://plato.stanford.edu/entries/parmenides/

32. Nirad Chandra Chaudhuri, see Appendix.

33. Scheduled Castes (SCs) and Scheduled Tribes (STs) are among the most disadvantaged socio-economic groups in India. https://in.one.un.org/task-teams/scheduled-castes-and-scheduled-tribes/

34. David Pocock, see Appendix.

35. Max Gluckman, see Appendix.

36. Adam Kuper, see Appendix.

37. On its first publication in 1973 Adam Kuper's entertaining history of half a century of British social anthropology, *Anthropology and Anthropologists: The Modern British School* provoked strong reactions. But his often irreverent account soon established itself as one of the introductions to anthropology. *Anthropology and Anthropologists* provides a critical historical account of modern British social anthropology: it describes the careers of the major theorists, their ideas and their contributions in the context of the intellectual and institutional environments in which they worked. https://amzn.to/36LwEiU

38. Edmund Leach, see Appendix.

39. *Politics, Law and Ritual in Tribal Society* compares nearly 40 case study societies, most of them in Africa, in their reconstructed pre-colonial

tribal condition, comparing their small-scale social relations to their large-scale social context. His approach manifests a strong interest in economy, politics, and social relationships. https://bit.ly/2SEIzqt

40. John Arundel Barnes, see Appendix.

41. James Mitchell, see Appendix.

42. The *Journal of the Royal Anthropological Institute*, formerly *Man*, was established in 1901 and is a quarterly journal with articles on all aspects of anthropology, as well as correspondence and a section of book reviews. https://bit.ly/3iBHgDb

43. An influential teacher or popular expert.

44. The North Central Province of Ceylon was the focus of a major civilization which flourished between the third century BC and the 12th century AD. The area is an arid plain where habitation is possible only with the help of an elaborate irrigation system; and the existing villages use the same irrigation works as the villages of antiquity. This 1961 book is a detailed analysis of how land was owned used and transmitted to later generations in one of these irrigation-based communities, the village of Pul Eliya. The main emphasis is placed on the way the ties of kinship and marriage are related to property rights and the practices of land use. The approach to this question provides a critical test of certain features of the theory and method of contemporary social anthropology. The factual evidence is very detailed, and the author allows the facts to speak for themselves wherever possible. https://bit.ly/3daqvOq

45. Meyer Fortes, see Appendix.

46. This collection by Claude Lévi-Strauss touches on a wide range of anthropological issues, including family and marriage, myths, and rites, the environment and its representation, and constraint and freedom. The essays encompass more than forty years of analysis and constrain arguments that are as relevant today as they were thirty years ago. https://amzn.to/30MZN9E

Jonathan Parry. Photograph courtesy Alan Macfarlane.

Jonathan P. Parry

Jonathan P. Parry (b. 1943) is Professor Emeritus, at the Department of Anthropology, London School of Economics and Political Science. Professor Parry has conducted field research in various parts of India on various different topics. His first study was in a rural area in the sub-Himalayan region where he focused on the classic anthropological themes of caste, kinship, and marriage. He subsequently worked in the city of Banaras where he studied the various communities of 'sacred specialists' in one way or another concerned with the 'business' of death-specialists who preside over rituals concerned with the disposal of the corpse, the fate of the soul, and the purification of the mourners.

More recently, Professor Parry has been doing fieldwork on industrial workers in the central Indian steel town of Bhilai (in the Chhattisgarh region of Madhya Pradesh) which was built on a 'green field' site with Soviet collaboration and technology in the late 1950s and early 1960s. The public sector Bhilai Steel Plant is now one of the largest steel plants in Asia, and has served as a magnet for a great deal of private sector industrial development. Part of the fieldwork has focused on shop-floor organisation, but much of it has been conducted in the ex-villages-cum-labour colonies in which the workers have their homes.

Professor Parry has also written more widely on the theoretical topics of death, the body, and exchange. His latest book Classes of Labour: Work and Life in a Central Indian Steel Town *(2019, Social Science Press) is a classic in the social sciences. The rigour and richness of the ethnographic data of this book and its analysis is matched only by its literary style. This magnum opus of 700 pages is an outcome of fieldwork covering twenty-one years, complete with diagrams and photographs, reads like an epic novel, difficult to put down.*

Death in Banaras *(1994, Cambridge University Press) is a study of Hindu death rituals and the sacred specialists who perform them in the Indian city of Banaras. As a place to die, to dispose of the physical remains of the deceased and to perform the rites that ensure that the departed attains a 'good state' after death, the north Indian city of Banaras attracts pilgrims and mourners from all over the Hindu world. This book is primarily about the priests and other kinds of 'sacred specialists' who serve them, about the way in which they organize their business, and about their representations of death and understandings of the rituals over which they preside.*

Caste and Kinship in Kangra *(1979) is a major addition to understanding the problems of social inequality and the nature of caste and kinship. A full account is given of the social structure of the region, emphasizing the continuity of principles, which govern relations between castes and relationships within castes. The ethnographic data bear in particular on: the nature of untouchability; models of caste ranking; the way in which 'traditional' family structures adapt to a diversification of the economy and the debate about the 'instability' of regimes of generalized exchange.*[1]

I

Alan Macfarlane (AM): Well, it's a great pleasure and privilege to have a chance to talk to Johnny Parry whom I have known for many years, but never had this kind of conversation with before. Johnny, tell me when and where you were born?
Jonathan Parry (JP): I was born in London in 1943.

AM: When in 1943?
JP: September.

AM: As an anthropologist you'll be aware that ancestors sometimes influence our lives and how far back would you like to go with your ancestors? Often people talk about their grandparents a little, a bit on either side or both sides. Should we go back any further or is that....?
JP: No. I don't know much about anybody any further back. Well if I start with my parents, my father came from a sort of well-heeled middleclass family – sort of aspiring to be really rather posh, sort of squirearchy at times. He was trained in the classics in Cambridge, became a civil servant, wrote novels, quite a lot of novels, died when I was very, very young.

AM: Did he write under his own name?
JP: Yes. He was called Dennis Parry[2] and he used to write these novels on trains as he commuted to his job. And my mother's family – it's not entirely clear because she was always very cagey about it. But it was a hypergamous union[3] that is they were much less posh, I mean sort of the lower fringes of the middleclass perhaps I think. Her father was always concealed from me as a child. He was a tailor in Swansea at a small tailoring business. But it took me a long time to discover this. And the marriage kind of broke up when I was perhaps six or something like that. So I was essentially brought up by my mother

This interview was conducted by Alan Macfarlane on 5 December 2008. The transcription for this interview was provided by Radha Béteille, for this volume. These interviews are available for viewing on:
http://www.sms.cam.ac.uk/media/1126936
https://www.youtube.com/watch?v=1reS6Aujpr0
https://www.youtube.com/watch?v=JWmHowCRinw

in what she regarded as straitened circumstances having made this spectacularly good marriage. In fact, they weren't straitened circumstances at all, they were just in terms of her expectations. So that's the sort of milieu that I....two upwardly mobile families but upwardly mobile from two very different starting points.

AM: Tell me something about the characters of your parents as you remember them. They must have shaped you in various ways, were they interested in books and ideas?
JP: Well, my father was. But I had extremely little contact with him you know, beyond the age of six. The marriage broke up in a good deal of acrimony and contact with my father after it broke up, before his death, was extremely fraught. I remember ghastly scenes of my mother on one side of the road and my father waiting in the car on the other side because they couldn't talk to each other. So, a small child having to cross the road.

AM: Were you the only...?
JP: No, I had an older sister, for whom it was all, partly because she was older, much more traumatic than it was for me.

AM: What was your mother's character with whom you spent a lot of time? How would you describe her? Is she still alive?
JP: No. She was, sort of difficult to say in a few words, but... she had left school. She had been a sickly child and left school at about 14 or 15, so was not at all well-educated in a formal sense. She was obviously extremely pretty as a young woman which enabled her to kind of make this marriage. The marriage was greatly disapproved of by my father's family. So, she had to contend with being cold-shouldered and treated as a social climber by her husband's family. She was someone who was always rather socially insecure, I think, that was a very important part of her personality and later in life she went to live in Italy on a small income. She could not afford to live in Florence as a lady than she could afford to live in London. She'd never learnt a foreign language before but she had good fluent Italian, she went to art classes. She had a sort of real dynamism; she was a strong-willed woman in lots of ways.

AM: Was she supportive of you through your growing up or more preoccupied with herself?
JP: No. She was supportive and kind of warm and affectionate. She had a much more conflictual relationship with my sister than with myself, who as I said took the divorce and so on much harder.

AM: Moving back – were there any of your grandparents you were close to at all?
JP: No. My mother's parents were dead by the time I was born. My father's father must have died at about the time I was born. Then my father's mother I did know as a child. She was a dragon! A frightening and tough lady!

AM: We usually go on to your first school. Do you remember anything about your first school? Where it was and...?
JP: I think I'd been at some nursery school before. But the first proper school – I was sent to a boy's prep school incredibly early. I think I might still have been six or just seven. And I can remember that this was in the aftermath of the divorce, and that home was not entirely comfortable and I was absolutely manic about learning to play cricket properly. You know I regarded this as a wonderful opportunity.

AM: So, you enjoyed that school?
JP: Yes. I mean on the whole I had a reasonably happy school life, academically not very distinguished or acceptable. I was a sort of sports freak! That's what I thought was serious! It wasn't until I was about 16 or 17 and started reading Bertrand Russell[4] essays and so on that I decided that I would like to be an intellectual which I think I thought probably meant wearing a black sweater and going to coffee bars!

AM: At that first school, were there...do you remember anything about the teaching, were there any teachers who...where was the school by the way?
JP: It was in Kent, but it burnt down after...with all the children inside it....after I had been there a couple of years. So, there was a dramatic fire. The school then temporarily closed down and it moved to Wiltshire.

AM: Were the children that might have been inside manage to get out?
JP: Yes. I remember being congratulated by the headmaster's wife because I thought the bell had gone so it was time to get up, so I was putting on my dressing gown and collecting my washing things.

AM: So, it was in the night?
JP: Yes, it was. It was in the night.

AM: Very dangerous
JP: Yes.

AM: But there were no teachers there who were going to spark your interest or imagination in your first school, the preparatory school?
JP: In an academic way I would say not. I was always interested in history, it appealed to my imagination. I remember from my later schooling, having a very good history teaching, enjoying history enormously but at that first school I don't really remember specific individuals as particularly charismatic teachers.

AM: Apart from sports, did you have any hobbies or particular enthusiasms as a child up to your secondary school? Did you collect butterflies or anything?
JP: I think I went through the kind of fairly standard range of hobbies – stamps were a great thing. I suppose I hadn't really thought of it – stamp collections may be somewhere in the origins of my interest in anthropology. These exotic stamps from South Georgia and Cambodia[5] and so on. I was always imaginatively drawn to these distant, exotic places.

AM: Where did you go after your preparatory school?
JP: I went to a conventional public school which was Sherborne in Dorset,[6] which I have jaundiced memories of. I remember the kind of alternatives for boys of my generation from that school were – you are going to be an army officer in Sandhurst or you go on to the stock exchange or you become a country solicitor. Few, few went to university. Going to university from that kind of school at that time basically meant going to Oxford or to Cambridge. If you couldn't get in you might consider Trinity College, Dublin, but you know they didn't send students to London or Reading.

AM: A rather snobby school.
JP: Yes, that's very much my memory of it, I may be doing it some injustice.

AM: You mentioned that there were teachers there who were beginning to enthuse you and can you remember any of their names?
JP: Yes. There was a man called Derek Jarrett[7] and there was a man called Graham Stephenson[8] both of whom taught history. And I remember them as the most charismatic teachers that I had, particularly Graham Stephenson. At the A level I did a special paper on the unification of Italy and that very much appealed to my imagination.
AM: This is all on the Arts and Humanities side, did you do any science?
JP: I left it after O level. I was never good at it. But as I say, I think I had an academically undistinguished school career, just good enough to just about scrape into Cambridge.

AM: Before that, other things at that school, had you developed beyond stamp collecting to anything else or was it mainly games, for instance music or drama or politics?
JP: Politics was always an interest and I was kind of interested in CND [Campaign for Nuclear Disarmament].

AM: In Sherborne?
JP: Yes. It was partly a sort of posturing, rebelliousness if you like. It was a very, very conservative institution at that stage. So, there was a group of us who vaguely entered the Labour party and the CND.

AM: Somewhat disapproved of by the local authorities?
JP: Yes.

AM: At some point I always ask about religion and it sometimes comes up later. A lot of your work has been in India and on aspects of religion. Were you particularly——as often as one goes through that great question on religious upbringing towards the end of one's schooling——How were brought up, as an Anglican?[9]
JP: I was brought up as an Anglican. I don't think my mother had the idea that it would be nice to go to church but it was the Tory party at prayer kind of church. I don't think she was very serious

about it though. When she lived in Italy, she flirted with Catholicism. I remember at about eight or nine I became a religious enthusiast for six months. I was actually confirmed in the Church of England. I mean the whole football team was confirmed there, you know! Since the age of about fifteen or sixteen I have been an agnostic. In later years I converted from being an agnostic into being a somewhat dogmatic atheist.

AM: Did you? When did that happen?
JP: I think that my personal attitudes to religion actually were hardened by doing the Banaras study.

AM: Shall we deal with it when we come to the Banaras study? And keep it on hold. That would be very interesting.
JP: Yes. Yes.

AM: What about any artistic or aesthetic side like music or painting or anything like that? Have you anything like that at all?
JP: My inclinations were always much more literary, so I was always interested in writing – the mechanics of writing. I dabbled briefly in trying to write poetry.

AM: On the mechanics of writing, which interests me too. You've written a lot and very elegantly, do you have any advice to people who write anthropology? What have you learnt?
JP: What would my advice be? Probably I should ask you at this stage to switch the camera off! I would say to young anthropologists 'don't read anthropologists who learn how to write on the whole'. I mean there are some very good ones, I think.

AM: Whom would you pick out?
JP: Evans-Pritchard,[10] Godfrey Lienhardt,[11] André Béteille.[12] Edmund Leach[13] wrote in a very direct and forceful, somewhat angular way. I would tell people still to do it in a way which got me into anthropology and read some of Bertrand Russell's essays. I think he wrote with extraordinary admirable clarity. George Orwell[14] would also be another excellent model.

AM: How do you actually write, technically, do you write on a computer, or have you always written on a typewriter or have you written by hand?

JP: At the moment, since computers came in, I write by hand, I put it into the computer, I print it out, I rewrite next draft by hand, and go on till I've got it in a shape that I think is more or less comprehensible, acceptable.

AM: Do you do it with all levels of things even if you are writing a short review or an article, do you write it by hand?
JP: Yes.

AM: Why do you do that?
JP: I like to have paper in front of me and to be able to go over the text and see if the sentences flow and I find it much easier to kind of pick out the balance of sentences with the paper in front of me. I mean why do I do it? I'm an old fogey, I guess that's the answer.

AM: Many people do and I do the same thing. How many drafts do you characteristically do with something you're writing? Do you correct it and type it in and then again?
JP: It depends on how pressed I am. Also, it depends a lot on the stage I'm at in an article or a chapter or whatever it is. At the beginning it's many, may be five or 10 and then the thing has taken some shape and I know more where I am going and how I'd phrased things before and so on and it goes much faster as I get to the end. So, I might do just a couple towards the end in the final sections.

AM: Well. Let's return to your career. You say you just did well enough to scrape into Cambridge. Why did you choose Cambridge? Just a random decision?
JP: My father had been here as I explained from that school at that time – you more or less went to Oxford or Cambridge or you went to Sandhurst. I did a series of entrance exams I think, I did one at Oxford, I did one here [Cambridge].

AM: Which College did you come to?
JP: King's.

AM: Some of my questions, I know the answers but I'm asking for the general public. Stephen Hugh-Jones whom I interviewed gave a nice account of his entry interview and so on. Do you remember yours? You came up presumably and talked to people here? Do you?
JP: Yes, that's right. I had entrance exams and interviews.

AM: Who interviewed you? Do you remember?
JP: I know that Edmund Leach interviewed me because I expressed some marginal interest in the possibility of doing anthropology.

AM: Do you remember your first encounter with Edmund at all? Later on he had a big influence on you.
JP: Later on. I mean I had no idea that this was such a distinguished man. I came here as a first year undergraduate to do arch[aeology] and anth[ropology]. This was an absolute revelation being taught by Edmund from a first week undergraduate. What I remember is the incredibly meticulous comments that you would get on essays and how we would sit in a room identical to this and he would pick books from his shelf and just say: 'Go away and read those. You might find these interesting'....

AM: Would you say he was a good undergraduate teacher?
JP: Brilliant, very charismatic. I did realize the commitment of time and effort that he must have put into writing comments on essays, giving us supervisions. He used to produce these sheets explaining what is complementary affiliation or...He was absolutely terrifically good.

AM: Did you ever find him uneven? Stephen told stories of asking his secretary how the weather was – was it stormy today implying that sometimes he was less even-tempered. You always found him equable in your supervision?
JP: As an undergraduate, yes. He was absolutely brilliant as an undergraduate supervisor and he was incredibly helpful when I was writing up my PhD. The period in between, my first year in preparation for fieldwork was more or less let us to sink or swim. I remember just before I went off to the field, there were these other senior graduate students who had all just come back from fieldwork like Maurice Bloch[15] and the Stratherns,[16] Jim Farris and Adam Kuper[17] – a very impressive bunch.

They had organized a seminar and Carrie Humphrey[18] and I were kind of beginners. We used to go along and I gave a paper at one of these seminars which was a critique of Edmund's argument in 'Animal Categories and Verbal Abuse'. And I showed it to Edmund and he was absolutely infuriated by it and kind of didn't talk to me for some time.

Then I came back from the field, the very first thing that I wrote was a critique of Edmund's introduction to 'Aspects of Caste'. After sometime that I had been back he said to me, 'You were showing me something, what is it you're writing?' With great trepidation I gave him this thing and I got wonderful comments back. 'This is terrific but the only problem is that you spent far too long trying to demolish Edmund Leach which everybody knows is rubbish any way!'

AM: Nice. You mentioned that there are a number of your contemporaries. As an undergraduate who, might we know, your contemporaries were? Carrie was there.
JP: Yes. I think there were four or five of us who went on from my year as an undergraduate. There was Carrie Humphrey, Jane Bramley, who became Jane Bunnag, who did fieldwork in Thailand and married a Thai, and subsequently moved out of anthropology. Enid Schildkrout[19] who did fieldwork in Ghana, myself and then there was Keith Hart.[20] Keith had done classics so was technically a year above us and then moved into anthropology. I did not know Keith personally, well, anyway, until later.

AM: Who were the teachers at that time? There was Edmund.
JP: There was Edmund, there was Tambiah,[21] who came when we were undergraduates. That was very important I remember. He was young. Originally, he was on a temporary contract and didn't know a lot of people in Cambridge so he was prepared to go out and have drinks with the third-year undergraduates. He was an incredibly good lecturer and it struck us that all the girls thought he was amazingly sexy.

AM: This was the period when the myths tell us, the staff and the students, no the higher ones, were much closer together and they used to go meet socially. Hierarchy was much less visible. Is that a true picture of it or the gap between say PhD students and undergraduates and even with the members of staff were much smaller and came later in large numbers?
JP: I think it doesn't entirely ring true to me. What I remember is having quite easy and informal contacts with Tambiah. And also Edmund who was very friendly. You know you could go for a drink

with Edmund. I don't remember if I ever got to know Meyer Fortes[22] or Jack Goody[23] until I became a graduate student and then there was the Friday seminar and people would have a beer afterwards. It would get much more informal.

AM: Again, I'm not sure if it was Stephen or someone who said that the rivalry between Fortes and Leach was so strong that students at that time were dissuaded——if they were a follower of one, they were dissuaded and didn't go to Jack's lectures because he was thought to be on the side of the devil.
JP: Yes.

AM: Was that true of your time?
JP: Yes. Very much true. I think Alfie[24] [Gell] has described this extremely engagingly in an interview he gave in the introduction to a collection of his essays that I put together after his death. He describes this extremely well that Edmund was Lévi-Strauss' Vicar on Earth and Jack Goody was the sidekick to Satan and so on. But it was sort of exciting you know in the sense that there was our team and there was their team.

AM: What were these people like as lecturers? I mean was Edmund a good lecturer as well a good undergraduate teacher?
JP: Yes. I thought that Edmund was a good lecturer. I think the good lecturers were, when I was an undergraduate, Edmund and Tambiah. Within the anthropology department I found that Ray Abrahams' lectures were the kind of lectures you needed to go to get an understanding of what was being said, take notes in. Actually, I didn't go to very many lectures at all while I was a student here. I did take studying anthropology seriously. How I spent my time was that Edmund would give me these books and I would go away and read them. I seldom went to lectures.

AM: One thing is why you came to do anthropology at all because it was a rather unknown subject? You had come from Sherborne to read Architecture and Anthropology – why was it that you chose Architecture and Anthropology? Do you remember?
JP: Yes. I think I do. I think there are a number of inputs. One input was that as I said earlier, I had been very struck by reading

these Bertrand Russell essays and there's this one collection called, *Marriage and Morals* the first essay which if I recall rightly starts out with Malinowski[25] and the Trobriands[26] [Trobriand Islands] that families aren't a God-given form in middleclass England. It struck me as such an amazing thought. Bertrand Russell was a serious influence. As a sort of lateish teenager I had been given a good deal of freedom to go off by myself in the summers. I had been to Turkey and I'd gone hitchhiking in Morocco.

AM: On your own?

JP: Yeah. On my own. I had come across Westermarck?[27]

AM: Oh yes. Edward Westermarck?

JP: Yes. I'd heard of it. It sounded terribly exotic. I didn't really know anything seriously about it, but the idea appealed to me. And then I think there was a straightforward pragmatic calculation that King's history had all these amazing well-read competitor students and that I had a better chance at getting into anthropology than I did history.

AM: What was King's like in those days? Can you give any straws in the winds as to what College was like? We are talking about '65?

JP: No. I finished in '65. I had come up in 1962. It was nice in the sense that....

AM: Was the Provost Annan?[28]

JP: That's right. It had the reputation of being much more liberal than the other colleges and that was very much valued. It had a kind of nice, relatively relaxed—— I'm hesitating here because certainly I did and I think and I made some good friends. Anthropology and girlfriends took me over, above all anthropology. A lot of my contemporaries wondered how we'd got in. It wasn't entirely relaxed, but I made some good friends, quite quickly. I very much appreciated King's and appreciated the fact that it was more liberal.

AM: Did you get involved in all those peripheral activities that undergraduates find compete with their work like acting, rowing or music...?

JP: No, I think anthropology took me over. Anthropology and girlfriends. But above all anthropology. It was the first time really that I had seriously engaged with intellectual activity and had begun to understand what it was about and I had got obsessed by it.

AM: What was it about anthropology that really gripped you? It sounds from the marriage thing, you come from a broken marriage, you've taken your own culture for granted and you've suddenly realized the relativism of your own world and you've started exploring other worlds?

JP: Yes, I think it was that. One of the things that has always appealed to me about it is that it is the idea that here is a discipline that in many ways is into relativizing and questioning the assumptions of other social science disciplines. And though I wouldn't have formulated it in this way at that stage, there is something about the democracy of anthropology – the whole lives of ordinary punters that anthropologists are interested in and it's difficult to think of other disciplines, except perhaps history that doesn't have live informants on the whole, but has that attraction.

AM: That is dealing with ordinary people?

JP: Yes.

AM: Let's move onto…you presumably did quite well in your Tripos, you got high marks, you worked very hard and so on. Did you get a First or…?

JP: Yes. I did disastrously in my first year because I completely ignored archaeology and physical anthropology which I'm afraid I was a terrible student at, not conscientious and so on. In the second and third years I got firsts.

AM: You won a State studentship or something?

JP: Yeah.

AM: Did you straightaway choose to work in India or did you have other places you would have liked to——how did you chose to do your PhD in India?

JP: I'm afraid this is a totally discreditable story. I had to fill in the forms when I was preparing for my final exams and I asked Edmund, 'What am I going to do?' He, sort of said, 'Well, why don't you go to India?' – which quite appealed to me. I did know I did not want to work in Africa. Intuitively, in some instinctive way, I wanted to work in a society with a rich recorded history and an encrusted ancient culture.

As we were talking about it at lunch, I've always been attracted to the possibility of working in South East Asia, and Japan at one stage appealed to me. I picked India because I needed to pick something very quickly and wanted to get on with revision.

AM: You just wrote India, you did not say south, north, east, west?
JP: No. I originally said that I wanted to work on polyandry in an area of the UP [Uttar Pradesh] hills and that indeed was what I thought I was going to do until I actually went to India.

AM: Had you even as an undergraduate imagined that you would be supervised by Edmund or was that a later decision? And you didn't choose India because you thought well it would be nice to go on with Edmund?
JP: Yes. I think that was very much a part of it. If I was going to stay on and do a PhD I wanted to work with Edmund. I really did not know very much about other university departments that I might've worked with. And I have said Edmund was an amazingly charismatic teacher. Just assume that I found the best by chance! Anyway, this was the thing to do.

AM: You mention that once you started on what was vaguely called the 'pre-fieldwork' training with Edmund, he more or less left you to your devices? There wasn't much formal instruction during that period – you went languages and things?
JP: Yeah. We were very much left to our own devices. I read a lot about India. I remember there was a seminar on councillors that Audrey Richards[29] ran with Adam Kuper, I used to participate in that. More or less, there was no guidance or training. I think we were given advice that we might read Laura Bohannon's[30] book on doing fieldwork, which I remember had something about the usefulness of tennis shoes.

AM: The water came out of the back! Famous advice!
JP: Yes.

AM: Did you get to know Audrey at all. What was she like, Audrey Richards?

JP: As an undergraduate I had been to seminars that she ran and this councillors' seminar. I never knew her terribly well. But she was warm and friendly.

AM: You presumably did six or nine months, six months before you went out to the field? How long did you spend in preparation?
JP: From October, which shows my extraordinary naïveté, till June.

AM: In the middle of the monsoon?
JP: I went to India during the hot season, the end of the hot season, by boat from Marseilles. I had seen 'Shakespeare Wallah'[31] and I thought that was still the way you got to India!

AM: Naïve in both senses – going by that transport mechanism! Can you remember arriving in India? Your first encounter with India?
JP: Yes. I landed at Bombay and was sort of really hit by the crowds and the heat. Then I took the train to Poona where I met up with a fellow Cambridge graduate student, who's a year before me, Tony Carter.[32] And Tony was very important in my association with India. Tony introduced me to village India. He then took me off for a few days or a week to stay in the village where he was doing fieldwork and took me around while he was doing it. This was an amazing confidence boost because this was a first-hand experience that you can eat yoghurt with your hands – the practicalities of how one might live in the field. I was exposed to it more, less immediately after I arrived. That was terribly important, giving a kind of confidence boost, yes, I can cope.

AM: But you didn't stay in Poona?
JP: No. I then went in the summer heat without any train reservations at all in a third class carriage to Delhi. After 36 hours. Then stayed in a small hotel and reported to M.N. Srinivas[33] at the Department of Sociology at the Delhi School of Economics.[34] During the preparatory year, André Béteille, who was then a Simon Fellow in Manchester, had come down to meet Edmund. I think he'd had lunch with Edmund. Then Edmund was busy and I had been detailed off to show André around for an hour or two.

Anyway, Edmund then twisted André's arm to become my supervisor while I was doing fieldwork in India – that led to a very important academic and personal relationship.

AM: Let's just take those two people among the most eminent Indian anthropologists/sociologists. Srinivas – how did you find him? What sort of person was he?
JP: I never got to know him particularly well. He was extremely gracious, helpful, good-humoured, but a little bit distant. I was a 22-year-old undergraduate and he was this very distinguished man, but helpful.

AM: Had you read any of his work by then?
JP: Yes. I'd read a collection of his essays and the Coorg monograph.

AM: It is difficult to summarize it, such a long and deep relationship as that with André, but he was your local supervisor and you've remained a friend ever since?
JP: Yes.

AM: We both know André quite well, but how would you describe André? And your relationship?
JP: How would I describe André! That's a fairly tall order.

AM: Yes, it is. Any anecdotes?
JP: Lots of anecdotes, but the first thing I would say about André is that he is a man of almost frightening honesty and integrity, I mean there is absolutely no bullshit, extraordinarily bright, quite reserved, it takes quite a long time to really get to know him, very loyal to his friends, and I think I would say really one of the most if not the most distinguished Indian social scientist of his generation.

AM: Of the whole world or in India?
JP: Of the world. Of Indian social scientists.

AM: That's what I thought, yeah.
JP: I mean I was thinking of diaspora Indians as well.

AM: I have always liked his work and been deeply influenced by it, but I always wondered if this dual ancestry that he has – I mean André Béteille – the French Indian and living with these two inheritances in a way which that must have influenced his interests in caste and class which he's mainly worked on. Did you notice that at all, anything of that in knowing him?

JP: I have always personally thought of André much more as a product of Calcutta and Bengal than I've thought of him as someone with dual ancestry; it is interesting that he has written about social inequality from so many different dimensions and so many aspects of it, but that one aspect of it that he has handled much less extensively than others is race. But I really think of André as a Bengali *bhadralok*,[35] a professor rather than a Frenchman in any sense at all.

AM: Well let's return to the fieldwork, did you, by this time, know where you were going? You were in Delhi.
JP: So I showed up in the Delhi School of Economics and went to see Srinivas and Srinivas asked me where I was going and I said ... and he said, 'Why on earth?' He was absolutely right, I mean, D.N Majumdar[36] had written a good book about this area and Majumdar had been a professor in that and he used this area as a regular place where his students and young lecturers went to do bits of ethnographic research. Srinivas's line was, 'You want to go to the hills that's fine, but of all the places in the hills, why pick there – it's just exotic neighbouring kind of little, little area. At least go round and look at some other possibilities'. And this seemed sensible advice. So, I picked out three areas that I would go around and look at. And I went to the first of them – Kangra,[37] which is where I ended up doing fieldwork. I thought this is great. Why go any further? And that's how I wound up in Kangra.

AM: Why was it great? What was great about it? Or describe your first impressions of it, if you can remember.
JP: It was this beautiful lush valley with mountains on one side of it going up 16–17,000 feet with snow and snow caps and it was September and it was very lush, there were streams and brooks. Physically it was extremely attractive. I found it very easy to meet a few people who were encouraging and suggested particular villages. Having abandoned the idea that I was going work on this polyandrous area, another interest that seems very promising is to work on local level politics. It was something that I had been very impressed and influenced by Freddie Bailey's[38] work which I had read in preparatory and my friend Tony Carter was also

very interested in factional politics which is what he was doing in Maharashtra.

My intention was that I would actually work on local level politics in Kangra and met some people immediately and was told about some villages where political rivalries looked interesting though I never wound up writing about that at all.

AM: Tell me something generally about the fieldwork. Any advice to younger anthropologists or whatever, many people find fieldwork a mixture of delight and misery, and ...loneliness and ...how did you on the whole at first ...fieldwork, was it mainly pleasurable and mainly okay or?

JP: I think it was the most difficult fieldwork that I have done. I have done fieldwork in two other areas subsequently and I think I probably got to enjoy it more as I got older, but I've always enjoyed it. I remember the first three months were somehow a terrific relief. I'd got a nice family that I was living with and the people seemed very friendly.

The next bit of time I remember as terribly traumatic. There was a general election going on and because I was interested in politics, I was making quite a lot of enquiries about what was going on politically in this place. And people suddenly became rather suspicious and I was reaching a plateau and I felt I was making no linguistic progress. I remember the period in between – three months and six months where I did find it very difficult and then I got into a kind of routine and was much clearer about what I was doing and got to enjoy it again.

AM: How long was that?

JP: The fieldwork. I was in India for two and a half years and I think I was in the field for about twenty-six months.

AM: By modern standards they rush them in three or four years.

JP: Yes.

AM: A long period.

JP: Yes.

AM: One of the changes in policy that students now seem to do characteristically shorter fieldwork.

JP: Yes. We were sent off in a much more open-ended way. Now there are research appraisals, X is going to work on notions of personhood or whatever and I went to the field with very vague ideas and I'm going to go and see what's there.

AM: Which do you think is the preferable or given the present circumstances there's probably no choice but do you think that old-fashioned way, is the same that I had, which was holistic, you studied everything and you find what was most interesting. Do you think that's still viable or...?

JP: I think it is still viable if people have enough time because they don't. I didn't really see any alternative – much more direct. And I think I was dead lucky in the sense that I wound up writing about caste and kinship though I hardly knew of Louis Dumont's[39] work when I went to the field and hadn't in fact read, I think it was published in French first in '66 which is when I was beginning my fieldwork. But André had been reading Dumont and would ask me questions and talk to me when I went to Delhi about Dumont's work. Somehow, I was collecting data that was relevant to Dumontian questions without ever having properly read Dumont. There was a kind of steer that I was getting.

AM: André's always been fairly ambivalent about Dumont's work. What is your ...he's a major overshadowing figure on subjects which you work on.

JP: Yes.

AM: Do you know him at all?

JP: I've met him a few times, I must have met him three or four times, but I wouldn't say that we had a personal relationship whereas the one I had with André.

AM: But as a thinker?

JP: Very highly, although he has become an increasingly unfashionable figure. But I remain in many ways quite committed to the Dumontian legacy. I think any Indianist of my generation basically has had their career and intellectual agenda set by Dumont. I think that he has been very unfairly criticized where he is actually right, where a lot of people it is conventional now to say that he was wrong and vice versa.

The bits of Dumont like the theory about the substantialization of caste which is still trotted out I feel is deeply problematic. I think that he was a powerful figure who represented to people of my generation the very exciting possibility of being able to bring together the very diverse studies that have been done in India and make sense of them according to a small set of unifying principles. There was a real excitement in this of being able to relate what Bailey was saying about Orissa with something that was going on in Tamil Nadu and to see variations on a theme in terms of these structuring principles.

II

AM: Your first fieldwork led to a PhD and a book. Can you briefly summarize what the problem was and what your answer to the problem was in that first work – *Caste and Kinship in Kangra*?

JP: It was an attempt to take off from Dumont, to demonstrate the pervasiveness of the principle of hierarchy and how hierarchical relations are not just a matter of relations between castes, but its penetration within castes, so that they order the texture of human social relationships from a very micro level to within the family; to relations within and between clans; marriage circles and so forth. And how the language of hierarchy is used to describe many other forms of social relationships.

And yet at the same time there is a countervailing force in the particular case I described ideas about equality rooted in notions of brotherhood, and how this social system works out – that would be one aspect of it. Perhaps the most important and interesting ethnographic bit was about marriage, particularly about systems of unequal marriage, hypergamous marriages, and how there are internal contradictions within the system that are continually threatening it with downfall which indeed, downfall does happen in marriage circles to be organized into egalitarian *biradaris* (brotherhoods) and how these in turn generate contradiction. It's very much as I can tell by that smile on your face, you're recognizing *Political Systems in Highland Burma*. It was very much influenced by that but it was also deeply influenced by reading of Lévi-Strauss's[40] *Elementary Structures of Kinship*.

AM: I am smiling because of that, but also because of something which you perhaps won't like too much which was the curious parallel between the beginning of our interview and where we got to now and anyone watching this interview will say, 'Well isn't he writing about his own childhood?'

JP: Yes, which was precisely why I mentioned the hypergamous marriage at the beginning. I am conscious of that. However, it's not the problem, I mean this has happened to me more than once in my fieldwork. I think I got interested in this problem, perhaps, though I wasn't aware of it at the time because of my own personal background. But it certainly wasn't the case that I decided to work on Kangra, because I was simply too ignorant to know that I was going to come across this kind of marriage system.

AM: It's the double thing as in your parents hypergamous marriage and stress you laid on class and inequality in your own family tree and background which pervaded your childhood a lot – snobbery and childhood oppositions between different social strata in England.

JP: Yes. That is exactly right. It had some resonance with me and perhaps that's why I wound up writing about it. But I have also to say that I did, as I said earlier, I did a lot of empirical work on local level politics and it was André who really discouraged me from pursuing that and writing about it. He basically said, 'You haven't got the kind of intellectual background to really write about this in a very good way'. I had been influenced by game theory stuff and André was a bit sniffy about it. He said that the stuff you're getting on kinship and marriage is actually much more important than your game theory. You do that and then maybe later on come back to the serious stuff of politics!

AM: Did you ever come back to it?

JP: No. I sometimes had fantasies about doing so, but I think André was dead right that I was sufficiently well informed about the literature on what I was doing with that data at that stage.

AM: Was there ever any difficulty about having a local supervisor or having a supervisor back in England? You didn't get contrary advice between the two? I suppose you didn't hear much from Edmund.

JP: No, I think one letter from Edmund in the course of two and a half years. I mean a very friendly letter and I had written a little piece about politics for the Indian journal *Seminar*. I had written a report on the election and the one letter I had from Edmund is that I sent him this piece when it was published. A nice short note, saying, 'Glad to see you're getting in print'. It was the time when Edmund was becoming Provost of King's and I'm sure he was fully preoccupied with more important matters.

AM: When you came back, do you remember students, people have a reverse culture shock when they come back to England, especially after such a long time – did you have any difficulties when you came back or was it a great relief or pleasure to be back?
JP: No. I think it was quite difficult actually. I came back and moved back to Cambridge. I really didn't like it at all and I very much valued my experiences as an undergraduate in Cambridge and got a lot out of it, but didn't like being back in Cambridge afterwards. It was partly because all my friends had moved on and the cohorts of people that I had got out of sync with. Carrie had spent a lot of time trying to get permission to get into the Soviet Union to do her fieldwork. She was still doing fieldwork. Keith's fieldwork had been much shorter. I didn't know people terribly well and in fact I went to live in London.

The other thing is that the period of fieldwork was over and there was an extraordinary hiatus in youth culture in Britain in '66. I came back at the end of 1968 and suddenly the world had changed and the political landscape had changed very much and it all felt quite alien.

AM: But how was Edmund? I think you had mentioned that he was very helpful when you were writing up, but you didn't go to writing-up seminars because you were in London or did you go to a few of those?
JP: As I recall there were not writing-up seminars at that stage. There were regular Friday seminars at which I remember I gave at least two papers.

AM: That really was the writing up seminar in a way, wasn't it?
JP: Yes. But it wasn't differentiated into a student seminar, so that one week there might be a graduate student, the next week there may be Clifford Geertz.[41]

AM: Do you remember anything about those seminars, were they lively, exciting occasions or bloodbaths?
JP: No. I do remember something about them. I remember them more in a way before I went to the field in that preparatory period as these ritual jousts. But then I was attached as I said as a student to the Delhi

School of Economics and somewhat to my arrogant British pride I was astounded by the fact that the Delhi School sociology seminars seemed to me to be better and more engaged and more articulate than the Cambridge seminars. I just assumed that the Cambridge seminars were pretty damned good. So, I think after that I always looked at the Cambridge seminars with a more critical eye.

AM: Did you do any teaching at this stage? Did you begin to do any supervising or anything either in London or Cambridge while you were writing up?
JP: While I was writing up Tambiah was running a South Asia class and he used to have a man called Roger Ballard[42] and I to help him. We used to go along to all the classes and it was a way of Tambiah sounding off recently returned fieldworkers.

AM: And the thesis wrote itself or was it okay and you didn't struggle with it too much? How long did it take you?
JP: I think I was quite slow. It took about two years and I found it agony, but masochistically satisfying agony.

AM: Agony because it just didn't come out right and writing is very tiring.
JP: Yes. Writing is difficult and a lot of data. I just do think, maybe you're somebody like Alfred Gell whose just perfectly formed elegant sentences came out. I have to struggle.

AM: Who were your examiners?
JP: Meyer Fortes and David Pocock.[43]

AM: Were they okay?
JP: Yes, they were absolutely fine and very complimentary. I remember the viva during which I was rather nervous and it was a slightly trying experience because Meyer sometimes used to speak in the way that he would write – long sentences, many parentheses. There were periods that in the viva I remember David would intervene and say, 'I think what Professor Fortes meant to say is…'!

AM: After that what happened, did you get a job straightaway or…?
JP: I had a job already. I think the truth is the only reason that I finished and handed in my thesis was that I'd had an interview at

Edinburgh and they had said, 'Well your thesis will be in by the time you start here won't it?' And I kind of naively took this literally that it had to be. I submitted it on the day before I went up to Edinburgh and started teaching.

AM: When was that? About '70?
JP: Yeah, '70 I think.

AM: How long were you at Edinburgh?
JP: Three years.

AM: Was that a good experience?
JP: It was a very pleasant experience. I liked the city of Edinburgh very much. I liked my boss.

AM: Littlejohn was it?
JP: Yeah. Jimmy Littlejohn. The department at that stage was not in a very good shape and I was actually quite glad to get out of it, not because it was unpleasant but because I felt that I would never actually do anything if I stayed there. And I moved to the LSE where the culture was you do the right things!

AM: So, you went to the LSE in '74?
JP: Yes.

AM: Describe the LSE. What was the LSE like when you arrived? It was the time that Maurice was obviously there.
JP: Maurice [Bloch] was there, headed at the time by Julian Pitt-Rivers[44] and Ioan Lewis.[45] There was Jean La Fontaine[46], there was James Woodburn.[47] Stephen Morris[48] was still around....

AM: Peter Loizos[49] had also....
JP: No, Peter was there. Peter was a colleague and friend from the start, Joanna Overing[50] joined the same year as I did.

AM: Alfie [Gell] wasn't there?
JP: No Alfie came later. Several years later.

AM: And Chris [Fuller]?
JP: Chris wasn't there.

AM: It's a difficult thing to talk about one's own department, but the LSE, I knew it just a bit before you were there and a few years before and there was Raymond Firth and Schapera[51] and people like that....It had already changed, but it still had James and others there. I don't know whether you want to talk about the LSE department later because it had the reputation that it was quite driven into several factions and oppositions.

JP: I'm quite happy to talk about it. But that's not how I perceived it. I perceived it as being very fortunate. There were intellectual tensions and some personal tensions but on the whole people talked to each other. I thought it was a very engaged intellectual atmosphere. David McKnight[52] was there. There were people who worked together more than other people. I can see there was a degree of apparent exclusiveness, but I didn't actually experience it.

AM: Well, you're a nice person Johnny! No one could take exception to you. As you know the famous kind of tensions between Ioan [Lewis] and Maurice [Bloch].

JP: Yes. That was certainly there. When I first went there was Maurice Bloch. Maurice was still quite junior then but it was more Maurice being kind of an iconoclast. I remember an early staff meeting where the convenor said, 'This is what we're going to do', Maurice bursting out, 'Convenors are just like postmen, they do what we say'. Something to this effect.... Julian Pitt-Rivers, altogether too patrician to get seriously upset by it, but there was a sort of jokiness about it.

AM: You were obviously taught a lot and supervised a lot. Do you enjoy lecturing, and undergraduate supervisions and seminars?

JP: I think what I enjoy most is undergraduate supervision, so I get quite a lot of, I put quite a lot into it, I get quite a lot out of giving lectures, but I do spend a lot of time preparing them or have done over the years. Graduate supervisions and PhD students, I think the truth is that I've actually got to enjoy it more over the years. Perhaps because I felt I had more time, or more confidence or whatever. You know the LSE for a number of years, almost all graduate students have had two supervisors and those who've worked in South Asia have tended to work with Chris Fuller[53] and myself and we've made a relatively harmonious team. I guess it worked quite well, particularly over the more recent years.

AM: How many PhD students have you had roughly, do you know?
JP: I think it's something between thirty-five and forty.

AM: And also the number you've taught Masters?
JP: Yes.

AM: And what about administration? Do you like that or did you do much of that?
JP: I did all the routine graduate admissions. I think I did four years altogether as the convenor which I did actually not like. I did not like it for different reasons than one often hears, I actually found my departmental colleagues were extremely supportive and nice and that was all fine. But I just hated dealing with LSE bureaucracy.

AM: It used to be quite a top down intrusive bureaucracy.
JP: Yes. The first three years I had as convenor we had an RAE [Research Assessment Exercise], we had a HEFCE [Higher Education Funding Council for England] inspections and evaluation reports which I found a terrible nerve-wracking strain. As the convenor you feel responsible.

AM: When was this, in the '80s?
JP: It would have been in the '90s and it was a time where departments were becoming 'cost centres', you ran your own budgets and so on.

AM: At what point did you get married? Was it when you had a job?
JP: Margaret and I were living together when I was writing up my PhD thesis. We had got married shortly after I had taken up the Edinburgh job and she moved to Edinburgh with me. We got married in Easter that year.

AM: She's a filmmaker?
JP: Yes.

AM: What kinds of films does she make? Anthropological type films?
JP: No. She is a documentary filmmaker and she's made films on a number of different kinds of issues, one kind of drama documentary and she did a series on public transport for Channel 4. I think the best way of describing it would be that they are all in some way politically engaged documentary.

My latest fieldwork has been in industrial central India and because of the stage at which the children were, like you've been going back every year to Nepal, I've been going back every year to various parts of Bhilai. And Margaret set up an access training programme for teaching documentary film to twelve local kids who wouldn't normally get a look in the media in India. She has developed an interest in that place and an independent circle of social contacts there.

AM: We will come back to Bhilai in a moment. But in between I don't know whether you went back to Kangra and then your next big fieldwork project was Banaras – how did you shift and at what point did you shift?

JP: I think I started the Banaras fieldwork in 1976. I went back, in '74 very briefly to Kangra. But the main purpose of that trip was to suss out the possibility of the next lot of fieldwork which was the Banaras fieldwork. How it came about that I shifted – I mean I've done this twice I felt I had written up what I wanted to say on Kangra and I felt it was time to do something different. If I went on working on Kangra I would have gone back to political interests that, somehow, I would spend the rest of my time either discovering how I was wrong or trying to justify how I was right. I made a fairly clean break and went to work in Banaras.

AM: When was that, when did you go there?

JP: I went there first in '76. Well I went to look at it and work out the possibilities in '74 and I started the fieldwork in '76. I went on working in Banaras and I think I had fifteen months to start with and I kept going back to it till the middle of the '80s.

AM: Can you describe what that fieldwork was about, what was the central theme and your views?

JP: It was a study of death. Banaras is a major centre of the death industry. People go there to die, they go there to cremate corpses, they go there to immerse the ashes of corpses cremated outside and it was the study of the various caste groups of mortuary specialists. It was the study of death as a living. It was also a study of practical representations of death and mortuary rituals. The book that resulted was predictably called *Death in Banaras* – it tried to handle these two aspects, death as a social organization and as a business enterprise, if you like. Death – it's symbolic and conceptual framework.

AM: How is it that studying death turned you from an agnostic to an atheist?
JP: I found the Banaras fieldwork incredibly interesting and very challenging. But I found a number of the ideas that I discerned as underlying as to what people were saying deeply disturbing and frankly personally unpleasant. If you were an old man, priests would be telling him that their son had died in some tragic circumstances and priests would be droning on about death and the fruits of *karma* and I found this personally unattractive.

AM: Edmund was always very often angry about particularly monotheistic religions of the West and the ideas and concepts of damnation and you shared that – a sense of revulsion, not shared in the sense that you took it from Edmund but you have a similar feeling. Was that your dislike of all religions or just the two main ones you had encountered – Christianity and Hinduism?
JP: It was obviously based on the two main ones that I had encountered. I am, anyway, as my story of how I came to be confirmed as an Anglican would suggest, 'religiously unmusical', so this innate predisposition to scepticism to rationalist thought.

AM: And you did quite a lot of work on the idea of gifts and debts in that fieldwork particularly? What was that about? What was the theme of that?
JP: Yes. It was sparked off by some fairly dramatic, and to me extremely interesting ethnography, about the remuneration of these priests which is conceptualized as a religious gift. It is not conceptualized as a handout. These gifts are held to embody the sins of the donor and to do terrible things to the recipient unless they pass them on which they can't afford because that's their living. They are caught in this terrible double bind. It started out with this ethnography which to me was extremely interesting and rather a touching personal situation of these mortuary specialists, but not only mortuary specialists in Banaras but also priests. And

that took me back to relooking at Marcel Mauss's[54] classic essay into more general considerations of the anthropological literature on reciprocity and so forth. And I think that I would modestly claim that one of the spin-offs of this was a re-reading of Mauss's essay, but was not quite conventional at the time, but Mauss's essay much more in terms of his thought about the evolution of society and the evolution of forms of exchange.

AM: But it also led into among other things the book you edited with Maurice Bloch on the morality of money and tell us about how that book which has just been very influential, occurred.

JP: Yes. We had done an earlier book *Death and the Regeneration of Life*. I think it was me who suggested that we do a repeat performance and these were based on London University inter-collegiate seminars. Each of them had about eight or ten essays. I now think that their main significance is that they were a sort of branding for LSE anthropology. Large numbers of the contributors were either from the LSE or had been associated with it. It got people talking together and putting together their ideas on a certain theme. And I think, that it gave for a time anyway, a certain profile to LSE anthropology that was relatively significant. It had an identifiable and fairly coherent conception of where anthropology was going. The two books were preceded by fairly lengthy introductions that Maurice and I wrote which tried to pull the essays together to say something more general with greater or lesser success! Somewhat to my surprise actually the *Money and Morality* book was and is still around and people would still read it.

AM: My students certainly do! It is always difficult to co-edit a book with someone else and Maurice is a lively mind. Have you always found it quite easy to work with Maurice?

JP: Yes. I haven't found it terribly difficult. There was no question of sitting in the same room and going over a draft with Maurice. I need to sit down completely independently and take the texts we're working on and try to write it by myself and then give it to him and he crosses it all out! But no, I don't remember any kind of occasions where we fell out or that it was particularly difficult. I remember on one or two occasions – the paragraph that I had spent the day crafting was rubbish! No, I don't remember it as difficult at all.

AM: We won't go over too many of your other colleagues but Alfie Gell whom I never had a chance to interview – what was Alfie like as a colleague?

JP: Alfie, he was lovely actually. He was a wonderful seminar participant, just so, so clever and quick and you'd sit in a seminar and Alfred would be drawing all the time. He would come up with wonderful portraits of James Woodburn and James Woodburn's beard and tangles and so on! [And I would think] how's this guy who hasn't been listening to a word and then the paper giver would end and Alfie would give this very long and incisive comment, terrific. I never worked with Alfred in the way that I worked with say, Maurice or Chris Fuller, but I always very much enjoyed him as a colleague. He's very much a kind of learned individualist – Alfie.

AM: Let us go on to your third piece of fieldwork which was again very different from your second – how did that come about and when did it come about – Bhilai?

JP: Again, I tend not to finish things until I somehow have to.

AM: It's like the PhD?

JP: Like the PhD. So, I needed to commit myself to a new project. Again, like Kangra, I wanted a shift of scene. André has been a big influence and for years has been going on at me, 'You really ought to take modern India more seriously'. This was one of André's big problems with Louis Dumont. I was sympathetic to the idea of doing something on industry. There were two very important influences. This was essentially a study of steel workers in a big Soviet built steel plant constructed on a green field site in central India. I wanted to do something on industry partly as a big break and partly because Alfred had a PhD student, Chris Pinney and when Alfred was ill at some stage I was involved in Chris Pinney's supervision.

Chris Pinney had been doing a study in a company town in Madhya Pradesh and had got heavily into E.P. Thompson[55] and so on. Chris was an influence and I thought that's really interesting.

But an equally big influence was Michael Taussig's book *The Devil and Commodity Fetishism in South America* where I was terribly intrigued by his decoding of the stories of baptism of bank notes of the devil contracts and so on – sort of proto-Marxian commentaries on alienism and commodity fetishism.

I felt that this was terribly fertile but Taussig's ethnography was not always of the richest and most detailed kind. This opened up a whole field that I would like to get into. I decided I wanted to do something on factory labour. I went in 1992 just to look around and it was Alfie Gell who suggested that I might look at Bhilai. I went to various places but Alfred who'd done work in the south, Adivasi tribal area to the south of that had been through Bhilai and spent a night in a Russian hotel or something had said, 'It looks really interesting'. I just went there for a day and thought I could really imagine making something of this, so that is why I went there.

AM: What was it like, what interested you and what was the theme of the study? Was it everything at this point, you went with the usual open-minded way?

JP: I'm afraid disgracefully, yes. And really the question in my mind was a very non-academic question. If you were somebody of my age and you've been a peasant in one of these small villages you would've lived through an industrial revolution in the course of your lifetime. And how would your world have changed? How would you think about those changes and what in fact happened to caste relations and kinship relations and was it any different from the way your parents had grown up – that essentially is the set of questions, it's terribly broad, but the set of questions with which I have remained. And it's gone on proliferating because I started out and I was mainly working with workers actually in the steel plant who are 'sort of' the aristocracy of labour. Then I realized that a public sector factory and I think there are very big differences with people working in the private sector in all sorts of ways. So, I felt I needed to do some work in private sector factories and I felt I needed to look at the bottom of the heap, informal sector, unorganized sector labour. It has gone on expanding.

AM: But it's continuing?

JP: It's continuing but I feel that I have got to an age where I have got to draw it to a close. I have written quite a number of articles about it but still other things that I want to write in an article form, but I want to get it together in a big picture in monograph form.

AM: Will that be precipitated by deciding on the next project which will force you to finish this project? Have you got another fieldwork?

JP: I'm afraid at my stage of life it's precipitated more by thoughts of aging. I mean I would love to do more fieldwork in a different kind of setting but I think realistically I have been going now since 1993, more or less every year and I just have incredible amounts of data about this place.

AM: It's time to get it altogether.

JP: Yes.

AM: There are one or two general things we've touched on religion, politics, we sort of touched on briefly, you were against the establishment personally – Sherborne, but that actually does relate to this last fieldwork because when you came and talked in Cambridge you were talking about a particular incident of someone who had been imprisoned and who was a friend of yours. Do you want to talk at all about that – this will go out to the world and it's your chance to tell the world about this incident or will you rather not?

JP: I'll say something very, very briefly about it. This is a man called Ajay. Ajay became my research assistant in Bhilai. He's Malayali, he comes from Kerala and his family had moved to Bhilai in the late 1950s, early 1960s, working class people at the fringes of the lower middle class. Ajay when I met him he had been an agent for a very small company in Calcutta selling gear boxes to the steel plant, hated the job, became my assistant, worked with Margaret, my wife, later learning as one of the students on her documentary film project. He got involved in the civil rights movement, documented some police atrocities and he was picked up, completely cynically, and put in jail for 93 days. Eventually they had to let him out without charges. What more to say about this? I mean I should say this is what is very important to my ethnography——has been the experience of working with research assistants of whom Ajay was one. He is still a very good friend of mine as is the person who in my second year in Kangra was my research assistant in Kangra.

I have worked with these people who have become extremely good personal friends and have generally been people with real intellectual interests, but not at all educated in formal terms and who've been extremely important to the ethnography I have been able to get.

AM: That's a nice tribute. On this last instance, certainly at one point it was considered that anthropologists shouldn't become too involved in local politics in the practical sense or interfere in any way as they were objective describers of situations. Has your view shifted on that or have you always felt that if you saw injustices you should try and do something about it?

JP: No. I'm very ambivalent about it and somewhat mistrust anthropology that goes over too much into social activism.

Partly because it seems to me that there is an incompatibility between the anthropologist/sociologist's task and the partisanship that is required of political activism. However, when your good friends, people in whose houses you have spent many months living, on whom in many ways the success of your project has been dependent and who you think are thoroughly admirable people, get picked on and incarcerated in jail, and all their friends desert them, what else can you do?

AM: I've got just one more question and then we'll see if there's anything I might've left out. You've been going repeatedly back to India over the last 30–40 years and watched a country in which at the Bombay stock exchange they were wearing *dhotis*[56] and there probably wasn't a stock exchange just bullock carts on the roads if you look at some of these early films in the '60s and '70s to what India is now. And many people comment on what is happening. What are your feelings about what is going to happen? Do you feel optimistic and enthusiastic about the dramatic transformation or worried about how things are going?

JP: It's interesting that your last question was about Ajay. And I think that had you asked me that question a year ago I would have given you perhaps a slightly different answer, but the answer that I give you now is that I feel deeply concerned about the proportion of the Indian population that are left out of all this and to whom the basic rights of citizenship are effectively denied – education, health etc. – and for whom the democratic system and legal apparatus does not work at all, so I feel a bit gloomy right at this moment.

The study that I have been doing is quite relevant to all this because what you have is a working class in a place like Bhilai, part of which is a real aristocracy of labour, that has essentially been bought off or enjoys very privileged conditions, upwardly mobile, decent education, extremely good medical facilities, but is not the same class as the informal sector labour in terms of its interests and way it identifies itself. It has no interest whatever in political action on behalf of the bottom of the heap construction workers and so forth. So, I feel a bit gloomy. It is all great, but for one-third of the population and that one-third of the population is not doing well.

AM: It's only a third of it, some people would put the ratio even higher. But we've covered many things and there are always things in a life that one doesn't cover, but is there anything that you would've liked me to have asked you about that I have conspicuously failed to ask?

JP: I don't think so.

NOTES

1. London School of Economics. 2020. https://www.lse.ac.uk/anthropology/people/jonathan-parry

2. Dennis Arthur Parry (1912–55) was a British novelist. He died early as a result of a road accident, and none of his books was ever reprinted beyond a first edition until Valancourt Books reprinted *The Survivor and Sea of Glass* in 2014–15. Parry was educated at Rugby School and King's College, Cambridge where he read classics. He then turned to law and was called to the bar in 1936, practising in the Chancery Division. He was rejected for military service because of poor eyesight, and became a civil servant in the Air Ministry and subsequently the Ministry of Defence. https://en.wikipedia.org/wiki/Dennis_Parry

3. Hypergamy (colloquially referred to as 'marrying up', occasionally referred to as 'higher-gamy') is a term used in social science for the act or practice of a person marrying a spouse of higher caste or social status than themselves.

4. Bertrand Russell, see Appendix.

5. South Georgia (Spanish: Isla San Pedro) is an island in the southern Atlantic Ocean that is part of the British Overseas territory of South Georgia and the South Sandwich Islands. The main settlement is Grytviken, Cambodia, also called Kampuchea, officially the Kingdom of Cambodia, is a country located in the southern portion of the Indochina peninsula in Southeast Asia. It is bordered by Thailand to the northwest, Laos to the northeast, Vietnam to the east and the Gulf of Thailand to the southwest. https://en.wikipedia.org/wiki/South_Georgia_Island & https://en.wikipedia.org/wiki/Cambodia

6. Sherborne School is an HMC independent full boarding and day school for boys aged 13–18 in Dorset. It is a school that first provided education to just a few pupils, as part of the monastery, before becoming a Free Grammar School in the 17th and 18th centuries. A school founded in its current guise in 1850, brought to life the vision of the Reverend Hugo Daniel Harper. https://www.sherborne.org/ & https://www.sherborne.org/about-sherborne/history

7. Derek Jarrett, see Appendix.

8. Graham Stephenson, GGS (1928–2017) was the head of the Sherborne School history department. He had been taught by A.J.P. Taylor at Oxford. https://www.questia.com/magazine/1P4-2033663391/diary-peter-oborne

9. Anglicanism is a Western Christian tradition that has developed from the practices, liturgy, and identity of the Church of England following the English Reformation. Adherents of Anglicanism are called Anglicans, or Episcopalians in some countries. The majority of Anglicans are members of national or regional ecclesiastical provinces of the international Anglican Communion. https://en.wikipedia.org/wiki/Anglicanism

10. E.E. Evans-Pritchard, see Appendix.

11. Godfrey Lienhardt, see Appendix.

12. André Béteille, see Part III, p. 93.

13. Edmund Leach, see Appendix.

14. George Orwell, see Appendix.

15. Maurice Bloch, see Appendix.

16. Marilyn Strathern, see Appendix.

17. Adam Kuper, see Appendix.

18. Caroline Humphrey, see Appendix.

19. Enid Schildkrout, see Appendix.

20. Keith Hart, see Appendix.

21. Stanley Jeyaraja Tambiah (1929–2014) was a social anthropologist and Esther and Sidney Rabb Professor (Emeritus) of Anthropology at Harvard University. He specialized in studies of Thailand, Sri Lanka, and Tamils, as well as the anthropology of religion and politics. Tambiah was born in Sri Lanka to a Christian Tamil family. He attended S. Thomas' College, Mount Lavinia for his primary and secondary education. After finishing his undergraduate education at the University of Ceylon in 1951, he attended Cornell University, graduating in 1954 with a PhD. He began teaching sociology at the University of Ceylon in 1955, where he remained until 1960. After a few years as the UNESCO Teaching Assistant for Thailand, he taught at the University of Cambridge from 1963 to 1972 and at the University of Chicago from 1973 to 1976. He joined the faculty of Harvard University in 1976. https://en.wikipedia.org/wiki/Stanley_Jeyaraja_Tambiah

22. Meyer Fortes, see Appendix.

23. Jack Goody, see Appendix.

24. Alfred Gell, see Appendix.

25. Bronisław Malinowski, see Appendix.

26. The people of the Trobriand Islands are mostly subsistence horticulturalists who live in traditional settlements. The social structure is based on matrilineal clans that control land and resources. People participate in the regional circuit of exchange of shells called *kula*, sailing to visit trade partners on seagoing canoes. In the late twentieth century, anti-colonial and cultural autonomy movements gained followers from the Trobriand societies. When inter-group warfare was forbidden by colonial rulers, the islanders developed a unique, aggressive form of cricket. Bronisław Malinowski chose to go to the Trobriand Islands, in Melanesia where he stayed for several years, studying the indigenous culture. Upon his return to England after the war, he published his main work *Argonauts of the Western Pacific* (1922) which established him as one of the most important anthropologists in Europe of that time. https://en.wikipedia.org/wiki/Trobriand_people & https://en.wikipedia.org/wiki/Bronisław_Malinowski

27. Edward Westermarck, see Appendix.

28. Noel Gilroy Annan, see Appendix.

29. Audrey Richards, see Appendix.

30. Laura Bohannan, see Appendix.

31. *Shakespeare Wallah* is a 1965 Merchant Ivory Productions film. The story and screenplay are by Ruth Prawer Jhabvala, about a travelling family theatre troupe of English actors in India, who perform Shakespeare plays in towns across India, amidst a dwindling demand for their work and the rise of Bollywood. Madhur Jaffrey won the Silver Bear for Best Actress at the 15th Berlin International Film Festival for her performance. The music was composed by Satyajit Ray. https://en.wikipedia.org/wiki/Shakespeare_Wallah

32. Antony T. Carter, see Appendix.

33. M.N. Srinivas, see Part II, p. 51.

34. The Department of Sociology was established by the University of Delhi in 1959 as a constituent of the Delhi School of Economics with the eminent sociologist Professor M.N. Srinivas as Head of the Department. To begin with, the Department trained students for two courses: M.A. and PhD. In 1966, a two-year course for the M. Litt. degree was introduced. This has been replaced since 1976 by an M. Phil. degree course of a year's duration. In 1968, the Department was recognized as a Centre of Advanced Study in Sociology by the University Grants Commission (UGC), the first Department of Sociology to receive this recognition and has continued to be a Centre of Advanced Study since then. http://sociology.du.ac.in/history/

35. *Bhadralok* literally, 'gentleman', 'well-mannered person', is Bengali for the new class of 'gentlefolk' who arose during British rule in India (approximately 1757 to 1947) in Bengal region in the eastern part of the Indian subcontinent. https://en.wikipedia.org/wiki/Bhadralok

36. D.N. Majumdar, see Appendix.

37. Kangra is a city and a municipal council in Kangra district in the Indian state of Himachal Pradesh. Historically it was known as Nagarkot. https://en.wikipedia.org/wiki/Kangra,_Himachal_Pradesh

38. Frederick George Bailey, see Appendix.

39. Louis Dumont, see Appendix.

40. Claude Lévi-Strauss, see Appendix.

41. Clifford Geertz, see Appendix.

42. Roger Ballard, see Appendix.

43. David Pocock, see Appendix.

44. Julian Pitt-Rivers, see Appendix.

45. Ioan Myrddin Lewis, see Appendix.

46. Jean Sybil La Fontaine, see Appendix.

47. James Woodburn is a British anthropologist and the world's leading theorist on egalitarian hunter-gatherer societies – the Hadza people of Tanzania. http://radicalanthropologygroup.org/person/person/180

48. Harold Stephen Morris, see Appendix.
49. Peter Loizos, see Appendix.
50. Joanna Overing, see Appendix.
51. Isaac Schapera, see Appendix.
52. David McKnight, see Appendix.
53. Chris Fuller, see Appendix.
54. Marcel Mauss, see Appendix.
55. Edward Palmer Thompson, see Appendix.
56. The *dhoti*, also known as *panche, vesti, dhuti, mardani, chaadra, dhotar* or *panchey*, is a type of sarong that outwardly resembles trousers. It is a lower garment forming part of the national or ethnic costume for men in the Indian subcontinent. The *dhoti* is fashioned out of a rectangular piece of unstitched cloth, usually around 4.5 metres (15 ft) long, wrapped around the waist and the legs and knotted either in the front or the back. *Dhotis* come in plain or solid colours, silk *dhotis* with embroidered borders are considered to be formal wear. https://en.wikipedia.org/wiki/Dhoti

Appendix
Biographical Information
(in alphabetical order)

NOEL GILROY ANNAN, BARON ANNAN (1916–2000)

Noel Annan was admitted to King's College, Cambridge, in 1935 to read History. He became a Lecturer of Politics within the Faculty of Economics, and was Assistant Tutor in King's College from 1947 to 1956. He was elected Provost in 1956. In 1966, Noel Annan left King's to take up the post of Provost of University College, London. He remained there until 1978. From 1978 to 1981, he was Vice-Chancellor of the University of London. Elected to the House of Lords as a Life Peer in 1965, he sat on many boards and committees. He was a trustee of the British Museum 1963–80 and of the National Gallery 1978–85. He chaired the Royal Commission on Broadcasting, which completed its report in 1977. https://bit.ly/3iKFFv4

ARISTOTLE (384–322 BCE)

Aristotle numbers among the greatest philosophers of all time. Judged solely in terms of his philosophical influence, only Plato is his peer: Aristotle's works shaped centuries of philosophy from Late Antiquity through the Renaissance, and even today continue to be studied with keen, non-antiquarian interest. https://plato.stanford.edu/entries/aristotle/

FREDERICK GEORGE BAILEY (1924–2020)

Bailey who published professionally as 'F.G. Bailey' and was known to friends and students as 'Freddie', was a British social anthropologist who spent the second half of his career in the United States at the University of California, San Diego (UCSD). He received his PhD in social anthropology from Manchester University, working under Max Gluckman, and is closely associated with the Manchester School of social anthropology. A prolific writer of some sixteen books in anthropology, he is probably best known for his studies of local and organizational politics. https://en.wikipedia.org/wiki/F._G._Bailey

ROGER BALLARD

Ballard did his B.A. in Social Anthropology in 1966 from the University of Cambridge and his PhD in Sociology from University of Delhi in 1970. He is the 2012 recipient of the Lucy Mair Medal for Applied Anthropology. His areas of specialization are Punjab (East and West), Afghanistan and the UK. https://grfdt.com

THAKKAR BAPA (1869–1951)

Amritlal Vithaldas Thakkar, popularly known as Thakkar Bapa, was an Indian social worker who worked for the upliftment of tribal people in Gujarat state in India. He became a member of the Servants of India Society founded by Gopal Krishna Gokhale in 1905. In 1922, he founded the Bhil Seva Mandal. Later, he became the general secretary of the Harijan Sevak Sangh founded by Mahatma Gandhi in 1932. The Bharatiya Adimjati Sevak Sangh was founded on 24 October 1948 on his initiative. When the Indian constitution was in process, Kenvi visited the remotest and most difficult parts of India and conducted probe into the situation of tribal and Harijan people. https://en.wikipedia.org/wiki/Thakkar_Bapa

JOHN ARUNDEL BARNES, DSC, FBA (1918–2010)

Barnes was an Australian and British social anthropologist. Until his death in 2010, Barnes held the post of Emeritus Professor of Sociology, Fellow of Churchill College. From 1969 to 1982, he held the post of Professor of Sociology at the University of Cambridge. https://en.wikipedia.org/wiki/John_Arundel_Barnes

GREGORY BATESON (1904–80)

Bateson was a Cambridge educated anthropologist whose life's work spanned and influenced many academic fields, including anthropology, communication, education, psychotherapy, and sociology. Using cybernetic concepts to theorize human–environmental interaction in holistic and recursive ways, Bateson developed sophisticated and continually evolving accounts of reflexive relationships among culture, consciousness, communication, levels of messages, social and biological contexts, epistemology, and learning. https://bit.ly/3nu9R12

CYRIL SHIRLEY BELSHAW (1921–2018)

Belshaw was a New Zealand-born Canadian anthropologist, and was professor of anthropology at the University of British Columbia (UBC) from 1953 until his retirement in 1987. Belshaw attended New Zealand's Victoria College where he received a M.A., prior to continuing his education at London School of Economics where he received his PhD in Social Anthropology. After finishing his education, Belshaw worked as a colonial administrator and economist in the South Pacific. https://en.wikipedia.org/wiki/Cyril_Belshaw

PETER LUDWIG BERGER (1929–2017)

Berger was an Austrian-born American sociologist and Protestant theologian. Berger became known for his work in the sociology of knowledge, the sociology of religion, study of modernization, and theoretical contributions to sociological theory. https://en.wikipedia.org/wiki/Peter_L._Berger

HOMI JEHANGIR BHABHA (1909–66)

Bhabha was an Indian physicist who is often considered the father of the Indian nuclear programme. Bhabha was born to a wealthy family in Mumbai. In 1927, he went to England at Cambridge University. Although he began studying engineering per the wishes of his family, Bhabha was quickly drawn to physics. Bhabha earned a PhD in nuclear physics in 1934. https://www.atomicheritage.org/profile/homi-j-bhabha

MAURICE BLOCH (B. 1939)

Bloch was born in Caen, Calvados, to Jewish parents Claudette (née Raphael), a marine biologist, and Pierre Bloch, an engineer. His grandmother was a niece of sociologist Emile Durkheim and a much younger first cousin of anthropologist Marcel Mauss. Bloch was trained at both the London School of Economics and Cambridge University. He has carried out fieldwork among irrigated rice cultivators and shifting agriculturalists in Madagascar, and in other parts of the world including Japan. Partly because of his French background he has combined British and French approaches and was instrumental in introducing the revival in French Marxist theory to British anthropologists. His interests have focused on the notion of ideology and he has written on ritual and language. He is now working on how to relate the findings of cognitive psychology with anthropology. Maurice Bloch has taught in the USA, France, and Sweden and is a Fellow of the British Academy. https://en.wikipedia.org/wiki/Maurice_Bloch & https://www.lse.ac.uk/anthropology/people/maurice-bloch

LAURA BOHANNAN (1922–2002)

Laura Bohannan née Laura Marie Altman Smith (1922–2002) is the pen name Elenore Smith Bowen, was an American cultural anthropologist best known for her 1966 article, 'Shakespeare in the Bush'. Bohannan also wrote two books during the 1960s, *Tiv Economy*, with her husband, and *Return to Laughter*, a novel. These works were based on her travels and work in Africa between 1949 and 1953. https://en.wikipedia.org/wiki/Laura_Bohannan

JOHANNES BRAHMS (1833–97)

Brahms was a German composer and pianist of the Romantic period, who wrote symphonies, concerti, chamber music, piano works, choral compositions, and more than 200 songs. Brahms was the great master of symphonic and sonata style in the second half of the 19th century. He can be viewed as the protagonist of the Classical tradition of Joseph Haydn, Mozart, and Beethoven in a period when the standards of this tradition were being questioned or overturned by the Romantics. https://www.britannica.com/biography/Johannes-Brahms

NIRMAL KUMAR BOSE (1901–72)

Bose was a leading Indian anthropologist, who played a formative role in building an Indian Tradition in Anthropology. A humanist scholar with a broad range of interests, he was also a leading sociologist, urbanist, Gandhian, and educationist. Also active in the Indian freedom struggle with Mahatma Gandhi, he was imprisoned in 1931 during the Salt Satyagraha. https://en.wikipedia.org/wiki/Nirmal_Kumar_Bose

NIKOLAY IVANOVICH BUKHARIN (1888–1938)

Bukharin was a Bolshevik and Marxist theoretician and economist, who was a prominent leader of the Communist International (Comintern). https://www.britannica.com/biography/Nikolay-Ivanovich-Bukharin

ANTONY T. CARTER

Antony T. Carter, Professor Emeritus received his MA from the University of Rochester and his PhD from Cambridge University. He has done fieldwork in India on rural politics, kinship and marriage, households and personhood. http://www.sas.rochester.edu/ant/people/emeritus/carter_anthony/index.html

NIRAD CHANDRA CHAUDHURI (1897–1999)

Chaudhuri was a Bengali author and scholar who was opposed to the withdrawal of British colonial rule from the Indian subcontinent and the subsequent rejection of Western culture in independent India. He was an erudite and complex individual. https://www.britannica.com/biography/Nirad-C-Chaudhuri

ABNER COHEN

Cohen is Emeritus Professor of Anthropology at the University of London. California published three of his earlier books: *The Politics of Elite Culture* (1981), *Two-Dimensional Man* (1974) and *Custom and Politics in Urban Africa* (1969). https://bit.ly/34zecax

SIR DOUGLAS BERRY COPLAND, KBE, CMG (1894–1971)

Sir Copland was an Australian academic and economist. He is remembered for his interest in the application of economic analysis to practical problems. Copland helped found the Economic Society of Australia and New Zealand and was the first president of the Victorian Branch of the society and the first Editor in Chief of its journal *The Economic Record*. It is said of him that he 'pioneered the development of the economics profession in Australia'. Douglas Copland was appointed a Companion of the Order of St Michael and St George (CMG) in 1933. He was knighted as a Knight Commander of the Order of the British Empire (KBE) in 1950. https://en.wikipedia.org/wiki/Douglas_Copland

FYODOR MIKHAYLOVICH DOSTOYEVSKY (1821–81)

Dostoyevsky also spelled Dostoevsky was a Russian novelist and short-story writer whose psychological penetration into the darkest recesses of the human heart, together with his unsurpassed moments of illumination, had an immense influence on 20th-century fiction. https://www.britannica.com/biography/Fyodor-Dostoyevsky

LOUIS DUMONT (1911–98)

Dumont was an eminent French sociologist and Indologist, was a towering figure in the fields of sociology and anthropology in the world. https://bit.ly/3llng9R

ÉMILE DURKHEIM (1858–1917)

Durkheim was a French social scientist who developed a vigorous methodology combining empirical research with sociological theory. He is widely regarded as the founder of the French school of sociology. https://www.britannica.com/biography/Emile-Durkheim

VERRIER ELWIN (1902–64)

Elwin was a British-born Indian anthropologist, ethnologist and tribal activist, who began his career in India as a Christian missionary. He first abandoned the clergy, to work with Mohandas Gandhi and the Indian National Congress, then converted to Hinduism in 1935 after staying in a Gandhian ashram, and split with the nationalists over what he felt was an overhasty process of transformation and assimilation for the tribals. Verrier Elwin is best known for his early work with the Baigas and Gonds of Orissa and Madhya Pradesh in central India, and he married a member of one of the communities he studied. He later also worked on the tribals of several North East Indian states especially North-East Frontier Agency (NEFA) and settled in Shillong, the hill capital of Meghalaya. https://en.wikipedia.org/wiki/Verrier_Elwin

EUCLID (C. 300 BCE)

Euclid, Greek Eukleides, was the most prominent mathematician of Greco-Roman antiquity, best known for his treatise on geometry, the *Elements*. Almost from the time of its writing, the *Elements* exerted a continuous and major influence on human affairs. It was the primary source of geometric reasoning, theorems, and methods at least until the advent of non-Euclidean geometry in the 19th century. It is sometimes said that, other than the *Bible*, the *Elements* is the most translated, published, and studied of all the books produced in the Western world. Euclid may not have been a first-class mathematician, but he set a standard for deductive reasoning and geometric instruction that persisted, practically unchanged, for more than 2,000 years. https://www.britannica.com/biography/Euclid-Greek-mathematician

SIR EDWARD EVAN EVANS-PRITCHARD (1902–73)

Evans-Pritchard one of England's foremost social anthropologists, especially known for his investigations of African cultures, for his exploration of segmentary systems, and for his explanations of witchcraft and magic. After studying modern history at the University of Oxford, Evans-Pritchard did postgraduate work in anthropology at the London School of Economics and Political Science. He then did fieldwork among the Zande and Nuer of what is now South Sudan. Two books about these peoples, *Witchcraft, Oracles, and Magic Among the Azande* (1937) and *The Nuer* (1940), made his reputation. In 1940 he and Meyer Fortes edited a volume of essays, *African Political Systems*, that revolutionized the comparative study of governments. He was knighted in 1971. https://www.britannica.com/biography/E-E-Evans-Pritchard

SIR RAYMOND WILLIAM FIRTH (1901–2002)

Sir Firth was a New Zealand social anthropologist best known for his research on the M⊠ori and other peoples of Oceania and Southeast Asia. https://www.britannica.com/biography/Raymond-Firth

EDWARD MORGAN FORSTER (1879–1970)

Forster was a British novelist, essayist, and social and literary critic. His fame rests largely on his novels *Howards End* (1910) and *A Passage to India* (1924) and on a large body of criticism. https://www.britannica.com/biography/E-M-Forster

MEYER FORTES (1906–83)

Fortes was a British social anthropologist known for his investigations of West African societies. After studying at the University of Cape Town in South Africa, Fortes received his PhD in psychology from the London School of Economics and Political Science (LSE) in 1930. In 1932 he turned from psychology to anthropology and studied under Bronisław Malinowski at the LSE. During 1934–37 he worked in Ghana and, upon his return, was appointed lecturer in social anthropology at the LSE. Subsequently, he was appointed research lecturer in African sociology at the University of Oxford. He was professor of social anthropology at King's College, Cambridge, from 1950 to 1973. Fortes's special interests were the political anthropology and kinship systems of various African peoples, especially the Tallensi. Most of his studies were conducted in nations along the Guinea coast of Africa. Among his major works are *The Dynamics of Clanship Among the Tallensi* (1945), *The Web of Kinship Among the Tallensi* (1949), *Kinship and Social Order* (1969), and *Time and Social Structure, and Other Essays* (1970). https://www.britannica.com/biography/Meyer-Fortes

CHRISTOPHER JOHN FULLER

Fuller is an Emeritus Professor of anthropology at the London School of Economics and a Fellow of the British Academy. He has studied and written extensively about the people of India, particularly with regard to subjects such as Hinduism, the caste system, and the relationship between globalization and the middle-classes. Fuller was a lecturer in the Department of Social Anthropology at the University of Manchester prior to holding a similar position as lecturer in anthropology at the London School of Economics between 1979–87. He was a reader in anthropology at the LSE between 1987–94 and has been an emeritus professor of anthropology there since 2009. Fuller's primary area of field research has been the state of Tamil Nadu, particularly between 1976–2001 at the Hindu temple in Madurai that is dedicated to Minakshi. His first fieldwork was among the *Nair and Syrian Christian communities of Kerala* in 1971–72. Fuller has also conducted fieldwork in Chennai (middle-class managers and software professionals, 2003–05) and on *Tamil Brahmins* (2005–08). Other areas of research have examined popular Hinduism and Hindu nationalism, the caste system and the history of anthropology in British India. Fuller was elected a Fellow of the British Academy in 2007. https://en.wikipedia.org/wiki/Chris_Fuller_(academic)

CHRISTOPH VON FÜRER-HAIMENDORF (1909–95)

Christoph von Fürer-Haimendorf or Christopher von Fürer-Haimendorf was an Austrian ethnologist and professor at the School of Oriental and African Studies (SOAS) at London. He spent 40 years studying tribal cultures in Northeast India, in the central region of what is now the state of Telangana and in Nepal. https://en.wikipedia.org/wiki/Christoph_von_Fürer-Haimendorf

SIR PATRICK GEDDES, FRSE (1854–1932)

Sir Geddes was a British biologist, sociologist, geographer, philanthropist and pioneering town planner. He is known for his innovative thinking in the fields of urban planning and sociology. He introduced the concept of 'region' to architecture and planning and coined the term 'conurbation'. Later, he elaborated 'neotechnics' as the way of remaking a world apart from over-commercialization and money dominance. https://en.wikipedia.org/wiki/Patrick_Geddes

CLIFFORD JAMES GEERTZ (1926–2006)

Geertz was an American cultural anthropologist, a leading rhetorician and proponent of symbolic anthropology and interpretive anthropology. https://www.britannica.com/biography/Clifford-Geertz

ALFRED ANTONY FRANCIS GELL, FBA (1945–97)

Gell was a British social anthropologist whose most influential work concerned art, language, symbolism and ritual. He was trained by Edmund Leach (MPhil, Cambridge University) and Raymond Firth (PhD, London School of Economics) and did his fieldwork in Melanesia and tribal India. Gell taught at the London School of Economics, among other places. He was also a Fellow of the British Academy. He died of cancer at the age of 51. https://en.wikipedia.org/wiki/Alfred_Gell

GOVIND SADASHIV GHURYE (1893–1983)

Ghurye was an Indian professor of sociology. In 1924, he became the second person to head the Department of Sociology at the University of Bombay. Ghurye was appointed as Head of Department of the Department of Sociology in Bombay University in 1924, and retired in 1959. The department was founded by Patrick Geddes in 1919. However, when Ghurye took it over, it was on the verge of closure. The department came alive once again with Ghurye, and now, Ghurye is regarded as the real founder and 'shaped' the study of sociology there from then on. https://en.wikipedia.org/wiki/G._S._Ghurye

SIR JOHN RANKINE (JACK) GOODY (1919–2015)

Sir Goody was one of the great social anthropologists and comparative sociologists of the twentieth century. It is not easy to summarize his contribution in more than twenty-five published books and many articles, as well as the effect he had on academic life as an innovative administrator. Jack Goody's father was a technical journalist and he grew up in Welwyn Garden City and then went to St Alban's School. He went up to St. John's College, Cambridge in 1938 to read English and was influenced by socialism and the literary criticism associated with F.R. Leavis. He was William Wyse Professor of Social Anthropology at the University of Cambridge between 1973 and 1883. https://www.therai.org.uk/archives-and-manuscripts/obituaries/jack-goody

ANTONIO GRAMSCI (1891–1937)

Gramsci was an intellectual and politician, a founder of the Italian Communist Party whose ideas greatly influenced Italian communism. https://www.britannica.com/biography/Antonio-Gramsci

PHILIP HUGH GULLIVER (1921–2018)

Gulliver was a Canadian anthropologist specifically in Oriental and African Studies, a Distinguished Professor Emeritus at York University and also a Fellow of the Royal Society of Canada. https://en.wikipedia.org/wiki/Philip_Gulliver

ALFRED CORT HADDON (1855–1940)

Haddon was one of the founders of modern British anthropology. Virtually the sole exponent of anthropology at Cambridge for 30 years, it was largely through his work and especially his teaching that the subject assumed its place among the observational sciences. https://www.britannica.com/biography/Alfred-Cort-Haddon

KEITH HART (B. 1943)

Hart is international director of the Human Economy Programme at the University of Pretoria and lives in Paris with his family. His main research has been on economic anthropology, Africa and the African diaspora. He has taught at numerous universities (including

Yale University and the University of Chicago), most significantly at Cambridge where he was director of the African Studies Centre. He has contributed the concept of the informal economy to development studies and has published widely on economic anthropology. He is the author of *The Memory Bank* (aka *Money in an Unequal World)*. One personal obsession has been the relationship between movement and identity in the transition from national to world society. But his written work focuses on the apparent impasse between the national limits of politics and the fact that the economy is now global. https://en.wikipedia.org/wiki/Keith_Hart_(anthropologist)

HERBERT IAN PRIESTLEY HOGBIN (1904–89)

Hogbin was a British-born Australian anthropologist. He conducted field work in the Solomon Islands and New Guinea. https://en.wikipedia.org/wiki/Ian_Hogbin

LEONARD TRELAWNY HOBHOUSE (1864–1929)

Hobhouse was an English sociologist and philosopher who tried to reconcile liberalism with collectivism in the interest of social progress. In elaborating his conception of sociology, he drew on his knowledge of several other fields: philosophy, psychology, biology, anthropology, and the history of religion, ethics, and law. Interested in the process of social change, Hobhouse tried to correlate such change with its contribution to the general advance of the community; he also studied the history of knowledge, morals, and religions in relation to social change. https://www.britannica.com/biography/Leonard-Trelawny-Hobhouse

SIR MICHAEL ELIOT HOWARD OM, CH, CBE, MC, FBA, FRHISTS (1922–2019)

Howard was a British military historian, formerly Chichele Professor of the History of War, Honorary Fellow of All Souls College, Regius Professor of Modern History at the University of Oxford,

Robert A. Lovett Professor of Military and Naval History at Yale University, and founder of the Department of War Studies, King's College London. In 1958, he co-founded the International Institute for Strategic Studies. Howard was described in the *Financial Times* as 'Britain's greatest living historian'. *The Guardian* described him as 'Britain's foremost expert on conflict'. https://en.wikipedia.org/wiki/Michael_Howard_(historian)

DAME CAROLINE HUMPHREY, BARONESS REES OF LUDLOW, DBE, FBA NÉE WADDINGTON (B. 1943)

Dame Humphrey is a British anthropologist and academic. Humphrey's PhD (1973) from the University of Cambridge was on *Magical Drawings in the Religions of the Buryats*, supervised by Edmund Leach. Humphrey has conducted research in Siberia, Nepal, India, Mongolia, China (Inner Mongolia), Uzbekistan and Ukraine. In 1966, she was one of the first anthropologists from a western country to be allowed to do fieldwork in the USSR. Since 1978 she has held appointments in the Department of Social Anthropology (Cambridge). Together with Urgunge Onon she founded the Mongolia and Inner Asia Studies Unit (MIASU) in 1986. She retired from her post as Sigrid Rausing Professor of Collaborative Anthropology, University of Cambridge in October 2010 and became Director of MIASU. https://en.wikipedia.org/wiki/Caroline_Humphrey & https://www.socanth.cam.ac.uk/directory/professor-dame-caroline-humphrey-fba

JOHN HENRY HUTTON (1885–1968)

Hutton was an English-born anthropologist and an administrator in the Indian Civil Service (ICS) during the period of the British Raj. The period that he spent with the ICS in Assam evoked an interest in tribal cultures of that region that was of seminal importance. His research work was recognised subsequently with his appointment to the chair of William Wyse Professor of Social Anthropology at the University of Cambridge and with various honours. https://en.wikipedia.org/wiki/John_Henry_Hutton

JOHN DEREK JARRETT (1928–2004)

Jarrett was an English schoolteacher, historian and writer. He was born at Whyteleafe, Surrey and served in the RAF during World War II before studying history at Keble College, Oxford. He is best known for his edition of *Horace Walpole's Memoirs of the Reign of King George III*, and perhaps for his, sometimes, acerbic reviews in the *New York Review of Books*. Jarrett taught at Sherborne School in Dorset until the mid-1960s, then at Goldsmith's College of the University of London for the remainder of his academic career. Around 1990 he retired to Cornwall to complete work on his Walpole masterpiece, which was published in 1999. He died at Truro in Cornwall. https://en.wikipedia.org/wiki/Derek_Jarrett

ADAM JONATHAN KUPER (B. 1941)

Kuper is a specialist on the ethnography of Southern Africa, and he has written widely on the history and theory of anthropology. https://en.wikipedia.org/wiki/Adam_Kuper & https://www.bu.edu/anthrop/people/faculty/a-kuper/

JEAN SYBIL LA FONTAINE (B. 1931)

La Fontaine is a British anthropologist and Emeritus Professor of the London School of Economics. She has done research in Africa and the UK, on topics including ritual, gender, child abuse, witchcraft and satanism. In 1994 she wrote a government report: 'The Extent and Nature of Organised and Ritual Abuse'. After teaching at King's College, Newcastle (1961, part-time), Lovanium University, Zaire (1962–63) and Birkbeck College (1965–68) La Fontaine was appointed Reader in Anthropology at the London School of Economics in 1968 and Professor of Anthropology there in 1978. She retired in 1983, being granted the title of Professor

Emeritus. Professor La Fontaine was president of the Royal Anthropological Institute from 1985–87. https://en.wikipedia.org/wiki/Jean_La_Fontaine

SIR EDMUND RONALD LEACH (1910–89)

Sir Leach was a prominent British social anthropologist, is known for his critical adaptation of Claude Lévi-Strauss's structuralist principles in the interpretation of myths and social institutions. His book *Political Systems of Highland Burma* (1954) became a classic in social anthropology. In 1953, Meyer Fortes, formerly of the London School of Economics and by now head of the anthropology department at Cambridge University, invited Leach to join his faculty. Thereafter, this university would be Leach's base of operations. From July to November 1954 he engaged in concentrated fieldwork in a peasant village in Ceylon, on the basis of which he wrote *Pul Eliya* (1961a). In 1960 he was elected Fellow of King's College, and in 1966 he became its Provost. He was knighted in 1975. https://bit.ly/2Fekdko

VLADIMIR ILICH LENIN (1870–1924)

Lenin, original name Vladimir Ilich Ulyanov, was the founder of the Russian Communist Party, leader of the Bolshevik Revolution (1917) and the architect, builder and first head (1917–24) of the Soviet state. https://www.britannica.com/biography/Vladimir-Lenin

CLAUDE LÉVI-STRAUSS (1908–2009)

Lévi-Strauss was a French social anthropologist and leading exponent of structuralism, a name applied to the analysis of cultural systems (e.g., kinship and mythical systems) in terms of the structural relations among their elements. Structuralism has influenced not only 20th-century social science but also the study of philosophy, comparative religion, literature, and film. https://www.britannica.com/biography/Claude-Lévi-Strauss

IOAN MYRDDIN LEWIS, FBA (1930-2014)

Lewis is popularly known as I.M. Lewis, was a Professor Emeritus of anthropology at the London School of Economics. He was educated at Glasgow High School before receiving a Bachelor of Science in Chemistry from the University of Glasgow in 1951. He proceeded to St Catherine's College, Oxford, where he obtained a diploma in Anthropology in 1952 with the aid of a grant from the Nuffield Foundation, and a Bachelor of Letters in 1953. He studied under Franz Steiner and social anthropologist Sir Edward Evan Evans-Pritchard, who was himself an authority on the Nuer and Azande people of South Sudan, as a graduate student – finishing with a doctorate in 1957. https://en.wikipedia.org/wiki/Ioan_Lewis

RONALD GODFREY LIENHARDT (1921-93)

Lienhardt was a British anthropologist. Born in Bradford, West Riding of Yorkshire, England, of mixed Swiss and Yorkshire parentage, he went to Cambridge University in 1939, where he read English at Downing College under F.R. Leavis until he was called up and became a transport officer, stationed in Africa. He was followed in 1946 to Downing by his brother Peter Lienhardt, who also read English and became an anthropologist. After returning to civilian life, Godfrey's academic interests were redirected to anthropology by an encounter with Edward Evans-Pritchard, under whom he subsequently studied at Oxford. His chosen field of research were the Dinka of southern Sudan, a people closely related to the Nuer studied by his mentor, (1947–50) and the Anuak (1952–54). His work on the former, culminating in *Divinity and Experience: The Religion of the Dinka*, is regarded as unsurpassed as a study of African religion. His central, ultimately Durkheimian, premise here is that religion is not reducible to a matter of beliefs and practices, but rather to a complex set of natural and social practices. His methodology shows an acute sensitivity to the dangers of translating key words in an indigenous lexicon concerning belief and religion, for example, into Western languages. https://en.wikipedia.org/wiki/Godfrey_Lienhardt

NIKOLAY IVANOVICH LOBACHEVSKY (1792–1856)

Lobachevsky was a Russian mathematician and founder of non-Euclidean geometry, which he developed independently of János Bolyai and Carl Gauss. Lobachevsky's first publication on this subject was in 1829. https://www.britannica.com/biography/Nikolay-Ivanovich-Lobachevsky

PETER LOIZOS (1937–2012)

Loizos was a social anthropologist chiefly known for a trilogy of books chronicling the turbulent history of Argaki, a Cypriot village that was home to his forebears. His father, a Greek Cypriot communist, left his Irish mother when he was two. The war played havoc with Peter's education and by the time he was 10 he had been to as many different schools. Finally, after the family settled at Herne Hill, he won a scholarship to Dulwich College. He studied English at St John's College, Cambridge, graduating with a First, then spent a year at Harvard, where he developed an interest in film and dropped out to complete a Master's in Communications at Pennsylvania University. Loizos had by then joined the department of Social Anthropology at the LSE, remaining there for the next 30 years. When he returned to Cyprus in 1975, he traced the Argaki diaspora, studying how people had coped with dispossession and exile, what resources they had deployed, and how they created new lives in such difficult circumstances. His work resulted in the book *The Heart Grown Bitter* (1982), and in another film, *Sophia's People*. The trilogy was completed by *Iron in the Soul* (2008). https://www.telegraph.co.uk/news/obituaries/9252965/Peter-Loizos.html

GEORG (GYÖRGY) LUKÁCS (1885–1971)

Lukács was a literary theorist and philosopher who is widely viewed as one of the founders of 'Western Marxism'. Lukács is best known for his pre-World War II writings in literary theory, aesthetic theory and Marxist philosophy. Today, his most widely read works are the *Theory of the Novel* of 1916 and *History and Class Consciousness* of

1923. In *History and Class Consciousness*, Lukács laid out a wide-ranging critique of the phenomenon of 'reification' in capitalism and formulated a vision of Marxism as a self-conscious transformation of society. https://plato.stanford.edu/entries/lukacs/

D.N. MAJUMDAR (1903–60)

Majumdar was born of Bengali parents. He obtained a first-class master's degree in anthropology from the University of Calcutta in 1924. The training that he received there was in both cultural and physical anthropology, and to the end of his life he retained a broad interest in both the physical and the cultural aspects of the science of man. A large number of his papers and two of his books deal with anthropometric and serological studies among the tribes and castes of Uttar Pradesh, Gujarat, and Bengal. https://bit.ly/30Oj0ry

BRONISŁAW KASPER MALINOWSKI (1884–1942)

Malinowski was one of the most important anthropologists of the 20th century who is widely recognized as a founder of social anthropology and principally associated with field studies of the peoples of Oceania. A prolific writer, he soon published reinterpretations of Australian Aboriginal data from literature then very popular in anthropological circles. These gained him a reputation and promoted his plans for field research, and in 1914 he was able to go to New Guinea. Six months' work among the Mailu on the south coast produced a monograph that, while lacking theoretical development, was sufficient – along with his study of the Australian family – to earn him a doctor of science (D.Sc.) degree from the University of London in 1916. When he moved to the nearby Trobriand Islands, where he worked for two years in 1915–16 and 1917–18, Malinowski's talents flowered. Living in a tent among the people, speaking the vernacular fluently, recording 'texts' freely on the scene of action as well as in set interviews, and observing reactions with an acute clinical eye, Malinowski was able to present a dynamic picture of social institutions that clearly distinguished ideal norms from actual behaviour. In later publications on ceremonial exchange; on agricultural economics; on sex, marriage, and family life; on primitive law and custom; and on magic and myth, he drew heavily on his Trobriand data in putting forward theoretical propositions of significance in the development of social anthropology. Yet, while very rewarding, his field experience had its strains. Writing in Polish for his own private record, Malinowski kept field diaries in which he exposed very frankly his problems of isolation and of his relations with New Guinea people. https://www.britannica.com/biography/Bronislaw-Malinowski

MCKIM MARRIOTT

Marriott is Professor Emeritus in the Department of Anthropology in Social Sciences Collegiate Division of the University of Chicago. He has done fieldwork in Uttar Pradesh and Maharashtra, edited *Village India*, and authored varied studies on rural social organization and change. He is concerned with formulating and simulating indigenous sociologies and psychologies in India, Japan, and other countries. https://bit.ly/2GN3tRB

PHILIP MASON, OBE, CIE (1906–99)

Mason was an English civil servant and author. He is best known for his two-volume book on the British Raj, *The Men Who Ruled India* (written under the pseudonym 'Philip Woodruff', the latter being his mother' maiden name), and his study of the Indian Army, *A Matter of Honour* (1974). https://en.wikipedia.org/wiki/Philip_Mason

MARCEL MAUSS (1872–1950)

Mauss was a French sociologist and anthropologist whose contributions include a highly original comparative study of the relation between forms of exchange and social structure. His views on the theory and method of ethnology are thought to have influenced many eminent social scientists, including Claude Lévi-Strauss, A.R. Radcliffe-Brown, E.E. Evans-Pritchard, and Melville J. Herskovits. https://www.britannica.com/biography/Marcel-Mauss

SIR ROBERT MAYER

Sir Mayer was a financier, philanthropist and patron of Britain's most famous youth concerts, which bear his name. He died 9 January at his home in London. He was 105 years old. Generations of English youngsters, including Queen Elizabeth II and her son and heir apparent, Prince Charles, became acquainted with classical music through the concerts that Sir Robert and his first wife, the former Dorothy Moulton, started in 1923. The first Lady Mayer, a soprano and former concert singer, died in 1974. https://nyti.ms/33D8mpe

DAVID MCKNIGHT (1935–2006)

McKnight was a Canadian-British anthropologist and ethnographer who specialized in the anthropology of Australian Aboriginal people, with particular regard to the tribes of the Cape York Peninsula. He conducted over 20 field trips among Aboriginal people in Australia from 1965 to 1999. He completed his B.A. in both English Literature and Philosophy from Bishop's University in Quebec in 1957. He went on to study in Great Britain, University College London, obtaining his M.A. degree in Anthropology in 1965 on African death cults. He then shifted his research focus to Australian Aboriginal studies, beginning with a first foray into field research in Queensland in 1965. He was hired at Edinburgh University as a lecturer in Social Anthropology three years later, and then moved to teach the same topic at The London School of Economics. In 1977 he earned his doctorate from London University with a thesis on the intricate marriage systems among the indigenous peoples on the Mornington Islands. He was appointed Senior Lecturer in 1982 and held that post until his retirement in 1997. https://en.wikipedia.org/wiki/David_McKnight

JOHN FRANCIS MARCHMENT MIDDLETON (1921–2009)

Middleton was a British professor of anthropology in the United States, specializing in Africa. He was director of the International African Institute in 1973–74 and in 1980–81. His work on the

Lugbara religion is considered a classic of African anthropology. Middleton was born and grew up in London, England. He received his bachelor of arts degree from the University of London in 1941. After World War II he returned to school and received his bachelor of science degree from Oxford University in 1949, and a doctorate in anthropology in 1953, also from Oxford. Middleton did his field work for his PhD with the Lugbara in Uganda, beginning in 1949. https://en.wikipedia.org/wiki/John_Francis_Marchment_Middleton

JAMES CLYDE MITCHELL (1918–95)

Mitchell was a British sociologist and anthropologist. After the Second World War he was appointed by Max Gluckman to the Rhodes-Livingstone Institute in Rhodesia (now Zimbabwe) and during the 1950s he often visited the University of Manchester as a research fellow. He subsequently followed Gluckman to Manchester in late 1965, to take up a chair in urban studies. Clyde Mitchell was interested in the study of social structure, conceived as the observation of regular patterns of social relations that are persistent over time. https://www.socialsciences.manchester.ac.uk/mitchell-centre/about-us/clyde-mitchell/

HAROLD STEPHEN MORRIS

Morris who spent most of his academic career at the London School of Economics (LSE) died on 26 September 1993. He published under the name H.S. Morris. He was married to the social anthropologist Barbara E. Ward. Morris wrote a book called *The Indians in Uganda – Caste and Sect in a Plural Society* (1968).

JOHANNES CHRYSTOSTOMUS WOLFGANGUS THEOPHILUS MOZART (1756–91)

Mozart was arguably the most gifted musician in the history of classical music. His inspiration is often described as 'divine', but he worked assiduously, not only to become the great composer he was, but also a conductor, virtuoso pianist, organist and violinist. Mozart's music embraces opera, symphony, concerto, chamber, choral, instrumental and vocal music, revealing an astonishing number of imperishable masterpieces. https://www.classicfm.com/composers/mozart/

SIEGFRIED FREDERICK NADEL (1903–56)

Nadel was an Austrian-born British anthropologist, specializing in African ethnology. In 1932 Nadel was awarded a Rockefeller Fellowship, allowing him to do postgraduate training in anthropological African field research. Nadel studied at the London School of Economics, supervised by Bronisław Malinowski and C.G. Seligman. Nadel was one of three students – the other being Meyer Fortes and Sjoerd Hofstra – to receive this fellowship, and they became known as 'The Mandarins', one of the first cohort of students to study with Malinowski. A closely knit group, all them planned on studying West Africa, and even travelled in the same ship from England to Africa. Nadel began his fieldwork in Nigeria in 1933 with the Nupe people of modern-day Nigeria. His PhD, completed in 1935, was entitled 'Political and Religious Structure of Nupe Society'. https://en.wikipedia.org/wiki/Fred_Nadel

JAWAHARLAL NEHRU (1889–1964)

Nehru, byname Pandit was the first prime minister of independent India (1947–64), who established parliamentary government and became noted for his neutralist (non-aligned) policies in foreign affairs. He was also one of the principal leaders of India's independence movement in the 1930s and '40s. https://www.britannica.com/biography/Jawaharlal-Nehru

GEORGE ORWELL (1903–50)

George Orwell, pseudonym of Eric Arthur Blair, (1903–50) was an English novelist, essayist, and critic famous for his novels *Animal*

Farm (1945) and *Nineteen Eighty-four* (1949), the latter a profound anti-utopian novel that examines the dangers of totalitarian rule. https://www.britannica.com/biography/George-Orwell

JOANNA OVERING (B. 1938)

Overing is an American anthropologist based in Scotland. She has conducted research on egalitarianism, indigenous cosmology, philosophical anthropology, aesthetics, the ludic and linguistics through fieldwork in Amazonia. She has extensively studied indigenous Piaroa people in the Orinoco basin of Venezuela. https://en.wikipedia.org/wiki/Joanna_Overing

TALCOTT PARSONS (1902–79)

Parsons was an American sociologist of the classical tradition, best known for his social action theory and structural functionalism. Parsons is considered one of the most influential figures in sociology in the 20th century. After earning a PhD in economics, he served on the faculty at Harvard University from 1927 to 1929. In 1930, he was among the first professors in its new sociology department. Later, he was instrumental in the establishment of the Department of Social Relations at Harvard. https://en.wikipedia.org/wiki/Talcott_Parsons

WILLIAM JAMES PERRY (1887–1949)

Perry usually known as W.J. Perry, was a leader in cultural anthropology at University College, London. Megalith culture, according to him, was transmitted to the rest of the world from Egypt. He was a convinced hyper-diffusionist and collaborated with Grafton Elliot Smith. He was also interested in the history of religion. His daughter, a chemist, Margaret, married the eminent physiologist, Professor Robert Harkness. https://en.wikipedia.org/wiki/William_James_Perry

JULIAN ALFRED LANE FOX PITT-RIVERS (1919–2001)

Pitt-Rivers was a British social anthropologist, an ethnographer, and a professor at universities in three countries. Julian Pitt-Rivers attended Eton College and Worcester College, Oxford. Through his work as an ethnographer of empathic considerations for cultural diversity, he rebelled against his father, a Moselyite eugenicist who was interned by the British government in the early years of World War II. Pitt-Rivers received his doctorate in 1953, which was derived from his fieldwork in Andalusia, Spain, that led to his publication of the classic anthropological text *The People of the Sierra* in 1954. The introduction was provided by his Oxford professor, E.E. Evans-Pritchard. He taught at the University of California, Berkeley and the University of Chicago. In addition, he taught at the London School of Economics and several universities in France, including the École Pratique des Hautes Études in Paris in what would later become the École des Hautes Études en Sciences Sociales. https://en.wikipedia.org/wiki/Julian_Pitt-Rivers

DAVID FRANCIS POCOCK (1928–2007)

Pocock was a British anthropologist whose main field of study was the people and diaspora of the Indian state of Gujarat, and in particular the Patidar community of that state. After early education at Highbury School, he attended Pembroke College, Cambridge, where he studied English Literature under F.R. Leavis. During the 1950s, he moved to the University of Oxford to take a PhD in anthropology under the guidance of Edward Evans-Pritchard. It was at this time that he began to translate the works of Emile Durkheim and he also conducted fieldwork in Gujarat, as well as among the Indian diaspora in East Africa and London. https://en.wikipedia.org/wiki/David_Francis_Pocock

ALFRED REGINALD RADCLIFFE-BROWN (1881–1955)

Radcliffe-Brown was an English social anthropologist of the 20th century who developed a systematic framework of concepts and generalizations relating to the social structures of preindustrial societies and their functions. He is widely known for his theory of functionalism and his role in the founding of British social anthropology. https://www.britannica.com/biography/A-R-Radcliffe-Brown

PAUL RADIN (1883–1959)

Radin was an American anthropologist who was influential in advancing a historical model of social structures based on a synthesis of approaches, including social theory, economics, religion, philosophy, and psychology. He pioneered in such important fields as culture-personality studies and the use of autobiographical documents. An accomplished linguist, he described a number of North American languages and advanced a classification scheme emphasizing their unity. https://www.britannica.com/biography/Paul-Radin

VIJAYENDRA KASTURI RANGA VARADARAJA RAO (1908–91)

Rao was an Indian economist, politician and educator from Tamil Nadu. He was a recipient of the Padma Vibhushan (1974). He served as a Union Minister for the Education in 1971, elected as member for Bellary in 1967 and 1971. He obtained a B.A and M.A in economics from Bombay University before earning another B.A from Cambridge. He was awarded a PhD in 1937 from Gonville and Caius College, Cambridge. He studied with John Maynard Keynes. Manmohan Singh, India's former Prime Minister credited him with being responsible for the high quality of economics education and research in India, by being the founder-director of the Delhi School of

Economics, the Institute of Economic Growth, Delhi and the Institute for Social and Economic Change, Bangalore. https://en.wikipedia.org/wiki/V._K._R._V._Rao

AUDREY ISABEL RICHARDS (1899–1984)

Richards was an English social anthropologist and educator known chiefly for her researches among several eastern African peoples, especially the Bemba. She did fieldwork in Northern Rhodesia (Zambia), Uganda, and the Transvaal. Among her subjects of study were social psychology, food culture, nutrition, agriculture, land use, and economic organization. She is best known for her book *Chisungu: A Girl's Initiation Ceremony Among the Bemba of Northern Rhodesia* (1956) – a pioneering study of female initiation. https://www.britannica.com/biography/Audrey-I-Richards

W.H.R. RIVERS (1864–1922)

Rivers was an English medical psychologist and anthropologist known principally for *The Todas* (1906), a model of precise documentation of a people, and the important *History of Melanesian Society*, 2 vol. (1914). https://www.britannica.com/biography/W-H-R-Rivers

JEAN-JACQUES ROUSSEAU (1717–78)

Rousseau remains an important figure in the history of philosophy, both because of his contributions to political philosophy and moral psychology and because of his influence on later thinkers. Rousseau's own view of philosophy and philosophers was firmly negative, seeing philosophers as the post-hoc rationalizers of self-interest, as apologists for various forms of tyranny, and as playing a role in the alienation of the modern individual from humanity's natural impulse to compassion. https://plato.stanford.edu/entries/rousseau/

BERTRAND ARTHUR WILLIAM RUSSELL (1872–1970)

Russell was a British philosopher, logician, essayist and social critic best known for his work in mathematical logic and analytic philosophy. His most influential contributions include his championing of logicism (the view that mathematics is in some important sense reducible to logic), his refining of Gottlob Frege's predicate calculus (which still forms the basis of most contemporary systems of logic), his defence of neutral monism (the view that the world consists of just one type of substance which is neither exclusively mental nor exclusively physical), and his theories of definite descriptions, logical atomism and logical types. https://plato.stanford.edu/entries/russell/

NICOLA SACCO (1891–1927) AND BARTOLOMEO VANZETTI (1888–1927)

Sacco and Vanzetti were two Italian immigrant anarchists who were erroneously convicted of murdering a guard and a paymaster during the 15 April 1920, armed robbery of the Slater and Morrill Shoe Company in Braintree, Massachusetts, United States. Seven years later, they were electrocuted in the electric chair at Charlestown State Prison. Both men adhered to an anarchist movement. https://en.wikipedia.org/wiki/Sacco_and_Vanzetti

HAROLD MALCOLM WATTS SARGENT (1895–1967)

Sargent was born the son of a coal merchant. As a boy he joined the choir at Peterborough Cathedral, studied the organ and won a scholarship to Stamford School. By 18, he was awarded a Bachelor of Music degree by the University of Durham. In 1928 Sargent became conductor of the Royal Choral Society, retaining this post for four decades until his death. Throughout his career, Sargent promoted British music. On one famous occasion, an air raid interrupted a performance of Beethoven's Symphony No. 7. Sargent stopped the orchestra, calmed the audience by saying they were safer inside the hall than outside, and resumed the concert. https://www.classicfm.com/artists/malcolm-sargent/guides/facts/

ISAAC SCHAPERA (1905–2003)

Schapera was a South African social anthropologist known for his detailed ethnographic and typological work on the indigenous peoples of South Africa and Botswana. His work was influenced by his instructors A.R. Radcliffe-Brown and Bronisław Malinowski, from whom he learned structural and functional analysis. He devoted much of his time to studying the Tswana, and his research covered most aspects of their life. His *A Handbook of Tswana Law and Custom* (1938) continued to be used by Tswana courts into the 21st century. https://www.britannica.com/biography/Isaac-Schapera

ENID SCHILDKROUT

Enid Schildkrout is Curator Emerita at the Division of Anthropology, American Museum of Natural History (Curator from 1973–2005) and was also Director of Exhibitions and Publications at the Museum for African Art from 2005–2011 Enid does research in Social Anthropology, Historical Anthropology and Cultural Anthropology and Art History. She has done fieldwork in many parts of Africa, focussing on Ghana and Nigeria, where her work has included studies of urban ethnicity, migration, and women and children in Islamic societies. She has also curated many African art and ethnology exhibitions on the art of the Congo and West Africa. https://www.researchgate.net/profile/Enid_Schildkrout

ARTUR SCHNABEL (1882–1951)

Schnabel was an Austrian pianist and teacher whose performances and recordings made him a legend in his own time and a model of scholarly musicianship to all later pianists. https://www.britannica.com/biography/Artur-Schnabel

ANIL SEAL

Seal is a Fellow of Trinity College, Cambridge. Together with John Gallagher, he is one of the founders of the Cambridge School of Indian History which has helped to transform the understanding of modern India. His pioneering work on the *Emergence of Indian Nationalism*, published more than four decades ago, has led to many monographs from this School by many of his erstwhile research students, now among the biggest figures in the subject. http://www.csap.cam.ac.uk/network/anil-seal/

CHARLES GABRIEL SELIGMAN, FRS (1873–1940)

Seligman was a British physician and ethnologist. His main ethnographic work described the culture of the Vedda people of Sri Lanka and the Shilluk people of the Sudan. He was a Professor at London School of Economics and was highly influential as the teacher of such notable anthropologists as Bronisław Malinowski, E.E. Evans-Pritchard and Meyer Fortes all of whose work overshadowed his own. https://en.wikipedia.org/wiki/Charles_Gabriel_Seligman

NARAYAN R. SHETH (1931–2018)

Sheth was known as a pioneering industrial sociologist. His doctoral thesis at MS University Baroda, *Social Framework of an Indian Factory*, was published by University of Manchester Press and triggered academic interest in labour relations and factory settings in India. https://archives.iima.ac.in/director/Prof-NR-Sheth.html

SIR GRAFTON ELLIOT SMITH, FRS, HFRSE, FRCP (1871–1937)

Sir Smith was an Australian-British anatomist, Egyptologist and a proponent of the hyper-diffusionist view of prehistory. He believed in the idea that cultural innovations occur only once and that they spread geographically. Based on this, he traced the origins of many cultural and traditional practices across the world, including the

New World, to ideas that he believed came from Egypt and in some instances from Asia. An expert on brain anatomy, he was the first to study Egyptian mummies using radiological techniques. He took an interest in extinct humanoids and was embroiled in controversy over the authenticity of the Piltdown Man. https://en.wikipedia.org/wiki/Grafton_Elliot_Smith

DAME ANN MARILYN STRATHERN, DBE NÉE EVANS (B. 1941)

Marilyn Strathern is a British anthropologist, who has worked largely with the Mount Hagen people of Papua New Guinea and dealt with issues in the UK of reproductive technologies. She was William Wyse Professor of Social Anthropology at the University of Cambridge from 1993 to 2008, and Mistress of Girton College, Cambridge from 1998 to 2009; Andrew J. Strathern is Andrew W. Mellon Professor of Anthropology at the University of Pittsburgh, USA. He received his PhD from Cambridge University and is an internationally recognized scholar and social anthropologist with a wide range of interests, including the analysis of political and economic systems, kinship theories, social change, religion and ritual, symbolism, ethnicity, legal anthropology, conflict and violence, the anthropology of the body, and the cross-cultural study of medical systems. He has carried out long-term fieldwork in the Pacific (especially Papua New Guinea), Asia (especially Taiwan), and Europe (with a focus on Ireland and Scotland) and continues an active research and publication program in these global arenas as well as others. He also conducts research in and teaches on contemporary anthropological theory, linguistic anthropology, and linguistic and social issues in Europe and globally. https://en.wikipedia.org/wiki/Marilyn_Strathern & http://www.anthropology.pitt.edu/people/andrew-j-strathern

JOHN MILLINGTON SYNGE (1871–1909)

Synge was a leading figure in the Irish literary renaissance, a poetic dramatist of great power who portrayed the harsh rural conditions of the Aran Islands and the western Irish seaboard with sophisticated craftsmanship. https://www.britannica.com/biography/J-M-Synge

EDWARD PALMER THOMPSON (1924–93)

Thompson was a distinguished British social historian and political activist. His book *The Making of the English Working Class* (1963) and other works heavily influenced post-World War II historiography. Thompson participated in the founding of the British New Left in the 1950s, and in the 1980s he became one of Europe's most prominent antinuclear activists. https://www.britannica.com/biography/E-P-Thompson

SIR EDWARD BURNETT TYLOR (1832–1917)

Tylor was an English anthropologist regarded as the founder of cultural anthropology. His most important work, *Primitive Culture* (1871), influenced in part by Darwin's theory of biological evolution, developed the theory of an evolutionary, progressive relationship from primitive to modern cultures. Tylor was knighted in 1912. He is best known today for providing, in this book, one of the earliest and clearest definitions of culture, one that is widely accepted and used by contemporary anthropologists. https://www.britannica.com/biography/Edward-Burnett-Tylor

JAMES L. WATSON (B. 1947)

Watson is Fairbank Professor of Chinese Society and Professor of Anthropology, Emeritus, Harvard University. He taught at the University of London School of Oriental and African Studies, University of Pittsburgh, University of Hawaii, and University of Houston, and, since his retirement, at Knox College. Among his interests are Chinese emigrants to London, the subject of his doctoral work and first book; ancestor worship and Chinese popular religion in present-day and in history; family life and village organization;

food and food systems in East Asia. He is best known outside academia for his edited book, *Golden Arches East: McDonald's in East Asia* (1997, 2006). https://en.wikipedia.org/wiki/James_L._Watson_(anthropologist)

MAX WEBER (1864–1920)

Weber was a German sociologist and political economist best known for his thesis of the 'Protestant ethic', relating Protestantism to capitalism, and for his ideas on bureaucracy. Weber's profound influence on sociological theory stems from his demand for objectivity in scholarship and from his analysis of the motives behind human action. https://www.britannica.com/biography/Max-Weber-German-sociologist

EDWARD ALEXANDER WESTERMARCK (1862–1939)

Westermarck was a Finnish sociologist, philosopher, and anthropologist who denied the widely held view that early humans had lived in a state of promiscuity and instead theorized that the original form of human sexual attachment had been monogamy. He asserted that primitive marriage was rooted in the needs of the nuclear family, which he considered to be the fundamental and universal unit of society. https://www.britannica.com/biography/Edward-Westermarck

JACK BUTLER YEATS, RHA (1871–1957)

Jack Yeats was an Irish artist and Olympic medallist. W.B. Yeats was his brother. Butler's early style was that of an illustrator. He only began to work regularly in oils in 1906. His early pictures are simple lyrical depictions of landscapes and figures, predominantly from the west of Ireland – especially of his boyhood home of Sligo. Yeats's work contains elements of Romanticism. https://www.tate.org.uk/art/artists/jack-butler-yeats-2178

WILLIAM BUTLER YEATS (1865–1939)

William Butler Yeats was born in Dublin. His father was a lawyer and a well-known portrait painter. Yeats was educated in London and in Dublin, but he spent his summers in the west of Ireland in the family's summer house at Connaught. The young Yeats was very much part of the fin de siècle in London; at the same time, he was active in societies that attempted an Irish literary revival. Yeats is one of the few writers whose greatest works were written after the award of the Nobel Prize. https://www.nobelprize.org/prizes/literature/1923/yeats/biographical/